The Mystery of Suffering
and the Meaning of God

The Mystery of Suffering and the Meaning of God

Autobiographical and Theological Reflections

ANSON HUGH LAYTNER

RESOURCE *Publications* · Eugene, Oregon

THE MYSTERY OF SUFFERING AND THE MEANING OF GOD
Autobiographical and Theological Reflections

Resource Publications
An Imprint of Wipf and Stock Publishers
199 W. 8th Ave., Suite 3
Eugene, OR 97401

www.wipfandstock.com

PAPERBACK ISBN: 978-1-5326-7554-6
HARDCOVER ISBN: 978-1-5326-7555-3
EBOOK ISBN: 978-1-5326-7556-0

Manufactured in the U.S.A.   JULY 9, 2019

To the wife of my youth, Vicki: What Rabbi Eleazar says in b. Gittin 90b.

To my late beloved wife, Merrily: Song of Songs 8:6. As my trainer in life's practicum, you worked with me for twenty-seven years to soften my edges, challenge my ideas, and urge me to be (more) introspective and better at communicating, but you left this world without giving me my graduation certificate.

And to my beloved wife, Richelle: For me, you are Proverbs 3:18,17. When you re-entered my life, you warmed my heart with your sweet soul, your glorious smile, and joyful presence. You thawed me out, helped return me to the land of the living and loosened me up physically, emotionally, and spiritually. You helped me regain my silly. For all this, you have my abiding love and devotion.

I can live with doubt and uncertainty and not knowing.
I think it's much more interesting to live not knowing
than to have answers which might be wrong.

RICHARD P. FEYNMAN, PHYSICIST
HORIZON, "THE PLEASURE OF FINDING THINGS OUT"
BBC TV, 23 NOVEMBER 1981

Contents

Permissions

PERMISSIONS

The following essays of mine explored many of the ideas and material now found in this book:

"A Healing Process in Jewish Theology: From Passivity to Protest to Peace," in *Loss and Hope: Global, Interreligious and Interdisciplinary Perspectives*, edited by Peter Admirand. London: Bloomsbury, 2014. Used with permission.

"At Home with Death," in *Drash: Northwest Mosaic*, edited by Wendy Marcus. Copyright © 2012 Temple Beth Am. Used with permission.

"Jewish Leadership for Interreligious Dialogue," in *Religious Leadership: A Reference Handbook*, vol 2., edited by Sharon Henderson Callahan. Los Angeles: SAGE Reference, 2013. Used with permission.

"Jews, God and Theodicy," in *Religious Identity and Renewal: Jewish, Christian and Muslim Explorations*, edited by Simone Sinn and Michael Reid Trice. Leipzig: Evangelishce, 2015. Used with permission.

Acknowledgements

A SPECIAL THANKS TO Bonnie Fetterman, Mary Jane Francis, Richard Gordon, and Jordan Paper for their absolutely essential editing of this manuscript.

Thanks also to these family members, friends, and colleagues who shared their comments and insights with me over these many years: Dan Allender, David Blumenthal, Dan Bridge, Shoshana Brown, Dorothy Bullitt, Deborah Cohen, Charles Davis, Atta Dawahare, Gene Duvernoy, James Eblen, Sol Ezekiel, Andrew Fenniman, Charlie Freedenberg, Abby Grasek, Joyce Greenberg, Richelle Harrell, Lesley Hazelton, Adrian Hill, Bruce Hosford, Bruce Kochis, Trudy James, Debra Jarvis, Anya Johnson, Tammy Kaiser, Michael Kinnamon, Merrily Laytner, Phil Levine, Suzi LeVine, Hubert Locke, Wayne Lubin, Barb Maduell, Marla Meislin, Jed Myers, Daniel Migliore, Ruth Morris, Marsha Olsen, Janet Parker, Julie Pfau, Judy Pigott, Kathryn Robinson, Stan Rosen, Judith Sanderson, Lee Seese, Ed Shields, Michael Trice, Helen Vandeman, Jane White Vulliet, and Elizabeth Wales.

Abbreviations

Bereisheet/Genesis	Ber/Gen
Shemot/Exodus	Shem/Exod
Yayikra/Leviticus	Vay/Lev
Bamidbar/Numbers	Bam/Num
Dvarim/Deuteronomy	Dvar/Deut
Yehoshua/Joshua	Yeho/Josh
Shoftim/Judges	Shof/Judg
1–2 Shmuel/Samuel	1–2 Shm/Sam
1–2 Melachim/Kings	1–2 Mel/Kgs
Yeshiyahu/Isaiah	Yesh/Isa
Yermiyahu/Jeremiah	Yer/Jer
Yehezkiel/Ezekiel	Yeh/Ezek
Hosheiya/Hosea	Hosh/Hos
Amos	Amos
Michah/Micah	Mich/Mic
Havakkuk/Habakkuk	Hav/Hab
Tehillim/Psalms	Teh/Ps
Mishlei/Proverbs	Mish/Prov
Iyov/Job	Iyov/Job
Eicha/Lamentations	Eicha/Lam
Kohellet/Ecclesiastes	Koh/Eccl
1–2 Divrei Hayamim/Chronicles	1–2 Div/Chr
Mishnah	*m.*
Babylonian Talmud	*b.*
Jerusalem Talmud	*y.*

Introduction

Each of us has a life story, a spiritual journey, something that we may return to time and time again as we age, and this book represents a significant portion of mine.[1] Only a portion because, first of all, I'm not dead yet so the story remains unfinished, and second, because as long as I am alive I am constantly reflecting upon and reinterpreting my story to better fit into my understanding of what past experiences mean in the context of my life in the present.

At the heart of my story is a period of ten years during which my family and I endured wave after wave of suffering, grief, and death. But at the same time, it is also a story filled with love and transformation. Although I hated much of the experience while living it, I now also embrace it because it made me who I am. Having lived through the trauma of those ten years, I now dwell in the life-after and continually reflect on how I came to be where I am today.

This book explores how I struggled with the issue of why bad things happen to basically good people, a topic known in the theological trade as "theodicy"; how I dealt with spiritual/emotional crises while braving many waves of illness and death; how I left old beliefs behind and began developing new ones that better addressed the experiences I'd had. These are issues at least as old as the book of Iyov/Job.

I try to do theology in a creative way, the way artists and poets and authors do their work. Were I a more gifted writer, I might have tried my hand

---

1. I think it is vitally important that we share our spiritual journeys with others, just as we routinely do bits of our life stories, because there is wisdom—and sometimes folly—in our travels and travails; information and ideas that may help others along their own paths of spiritual development. Part of the Bible's enduring appeal, I think, is that it offers stories of people in whose lives God apparently played a major role and in which, unlike real life, we are told exactly how God participated in each story.

at fiction in order to express my ideas through the characters and events of a novel. (More people probably read and learn theology from Dostoyevsky or Wiesel—or even Brown's *The Da Vinci Code*—than Tillich, Thich Nhat Hạnh, Barth, Buber, and Heschel combined!) My creative way to do theology is to make an explicit connection between my ideas, the work that I did, and my life.

The late Speaker of the U.S. House of Representatives, Tip O'Neill, once said that all politics is local. Just as surely, all theology is personal. By this I mean that there are complex personal factors—psychological make-up, personality, stage of life, past experiences, cultural context, and current situation—that provide the shifting sands upon which any theology is built. But just as politicians prefer to obfuscate the personal motives underlying their decisions with grandiloquent rhetoric, so too do theologians generally cloak the personal roots of their theologies with dubious certainties. Instead, I try to keep my theology personal and rooted in my experiences.

As I said at the very beginning, this book is my attempt to make sense of those recurring waves of disease, dying, and death that washed over me and my family, leaving us gasping for meaning and dazed with pain. Of course, our family's experience is not unique. Other people have had life's events hit them far worse and I almost feel guilty *kvetching* (complaining) about what we've gone through. Perhaps our experience is more compact and intense than that of other folk, but it is not so special.

Death, as it is so often blandly asserted, is just a part of life. As are pain and suffering. And happiness and joy too—but who complains about these? In truth, words cannot begin to convey the depth of feeling one has when in the thick of things, or the dark thoughts that these sorts of experiences can engender: "Why me?" "Why her?" "Why is God doing this to us?" "What did we do to deserve this?" "Why go on living?"

These are the kinds of questions that suffering raises for many people. They are the very questions that Iyov (Job) asked. They can haunt one's nights, sliding into one's consciousness between the ticks of the clock in the wee early hours, rousing one with an ache in the stomach, or with a troubling dream, or in an anxious sweat. Many people prefer, I think, to go for years without truly contemplating these questions, only to be violently confronted by them at a time of crisis and loss, be it love, health, career, or the death of someone beloved. At one time or another, almost all of us are compelled by life's events to struggle to find meaning in what life throws our way, for better or for worse. We do so when we marvel at a birth or wonder about love, when we rage against disease or grieve over our dead.

These questions came to a personal head as I tried to make sense of the suffering my family had endured. What meaning is there in suffering, and how does it connect with God? For answers, I studied the book of Iyov intensively and then contemplated how its messages applied to my life. Then I wrote and rewrote over a fifteen-year period. The result is what you have before you—and still it remains a work in process!

I begin this book with a detailed analysis of the book of Iyov. (Once you get through that study, the rest of the book is a much easier read.) This chapter is followed by a mix of personal reminisences and theological reflections on the topics of suffering, prayer, God-concepts, revelation, and how best to live together. I share my stories and reflections with you not because I am a paragon of faith, but in the hope whatever wisdom I have acquired as a result of this dark encounter may be of benefit to you as well.

For someone else, it might have been quite logical to ask, "Why believe in God in the first place, and how much more so given all that your family had gone through?" But for me this was never an option because, owing to a mystical experience I had as a young man, I know there is a God, but like Iyov, I just wonder what on earth S/He/It does.

Chapter 1

Trying to Understand the Book of Iyov (Job)

"But whence does wisdom come? / Where is the source of understanding?" (Iyov 28:20)

I   THE LAW-COURT PATTERN OF PRAYER

BAD THINGS HAVE ALWAYS happened to basically good people and, from time immemorial, the experience of suffering has raised serious questions about God's justice and goodness, God's presence and reliability, and about God's willingness or ability to intervene.

While the justifications of God's ways are many, one type of response stands out as a particularly—and perhaps uniquely—Jewish way of dealing with theodicy: that of arguing with God.[1] In this tradition, an aggrieved person pursues the path of protest to God and against God regarding apparent injustice and perceived divine indifference (or even hostility) by setting his/her protest in the context of a court of law and employing the law-court pattern of prayer.[2]

---

1. For more on the tradition of protest in Jewish culture, see Laytner, *Arguing with God* and Weiss, *Pious Irreverence*. The pioneering work in this field is Olsvanger, *Contentions with God*.

2. Biblical and liturgical scholars have identified the various components of the

In the law-court pattern of prayer, the people Yisrael (Israel), or its representative, takes God to task, appealing to God the judge against God the defendant, with the expectation that once all the facts are clearly presented and the case argued, God the judge will rule in favor of the plaintiff and thus compel God the defendant to "cease and desist" hostilities or "make restitution" by intervening. Avraham (Abraham), Moshe (Moses), Eliyahu (Elijah), Yermiyahu (Jeremiah), certain *Tehillim* (the psalms of lament), and *Eichah* (Lamentations) all utilize this form of prayer.

The book of Iyov (Job) represents the apex of the law-court motif in the Tanakh (the Jewish Bible) because the legal dispute pervades the entire book.[3] The law-court motif also provides much of the structure to the disputation and offers the reader (the ancient reader, at least) a visceral connection to the story's message.

Here is the "logic" of the law-court motif in the book of Iyov:

- The foundational premise in the book is that the world is governed by a divine sense of order.

- This order is based on justice, which applies both to God and humankind as part of a covenantal relationship. If God were above justice, God could not have been challenged in court by Iyov.

- People (in this context, Jews) generally perceive this order in the form of divine reward and punishment (i.e., retributive justice). Iyov's

---

law-court pattern of prayer as follows:

- An address, usually in second person singular, to God the judge;
- A presentation of the facts of the case and the nature of the complaint being brought against God the defendant; and
- A concluding petition or request made by the plaintiff (Yisrael or its representative).
- Sometimes a fourth component may follow, namely, a divine response to the petition.

See Gemser, "Rîb," 126; Ullendorf, "Thought Categories," 279; Heinemann, *Prayer in the Talmud*, 207; Blank, "Prophet as Paradigm," 25.

3. See chapters 9, 13, 23, and 31 in particular. Roberts, "Job's Summons," 161–62, argues that Iyov is innovative in his use of the law-court motif because, rather than use it as a metaphor, he actually employs it: "One can see what Job has done to the metaphor. He has simply transferred it, untranslated, out of the realm of metaphor into that of literal prose. While traditional language spoke metaphorically of God entering into judgment with man, Job pleads that he literally do so in a tangible, equitable fashion." I would suggest that the law-court pattern of prayer is much more than metaphor for those who used it in their time of distress. It was utilized as a means of compelling God's attention and, hopefully, intervention—just as it was in Iyov's case.

2

friends affirm this directly, Iyov does so backhandedly through his legal protest, and God confirms it in the epilogue.

- Unwarranted or undue punishment (divine judgments) may be appealed as in a legal setting, in which God is both the defendant and judge. Such appeals may be lodged, and God is assumed to be a fair and unbiased judge, precisely because God is, or has chosen to be, subordinate to this justice-based order.

- God's appearance in court therefore follows "logically" as a consequence of Iyov's legally binding oaths.

In the book of Iyov, the author(s) utilizes the law-court motif to dramatically challenge the dominant theodicy of its time and then, through God's appearance in the story, to propose a startling new understanding of the meaning of suffering as it relates to divine justice.

II THE LEGAL ARGUMENT IN IYOV'S SPEECHES

As it has come down to us, the book is in the form of multiple dialogues, first between God and the Adversary (*HaSattan*), then between Iyov and his friends and Elihu, and finally between Iyov and God. While the prologue in heaven featuring the dialogue between God and *HaSattan* makes us privy to information that Iyov and his friends do not have—that all that is about to transpire is but a test of his faithfulness—the core of the book, the dialogue or disputation between Iyov and his friends, stands well on its own. Typically, this part of the book has been divided into three cycles of dialogue between Iyov and his friends (chapters 4–27).[4] Various scholars have observed that the legal motif propels the disputation along and provides the drama in the story.[5] Indeed, if one takes Iyov's various speeches

---

4. The third cycle is incomplete, with the expected speech of Tzophar being replaced by the so-called wisdom poem of chapter 28. For a summary of current scholarly perspectives on chapter 28, see Newsom, *Book of Job*, 169–70. See Clines, "Arguments of Job's Three Friends," 209–10, for a summary of the distinct points of views of the three friends.

5. See Habel, *Book of Job*, 54–57. John. E. Hartley traces a similar progression in Iyov's laments and speeches from chapter 3 to 26/27 (the final speech of dialogue) in "From Lament to Oath," especially 89–97. See also Zuckerman, *Job the Silent*, 104–17. Claus Westermann does the same in *Structure of the Book of Job*, 17–30. Crenshaw, *Reading Job*, 20, also notes the legal motif and points to several other studies of the legal motif in Iyov, including Sutherland, *Putting God on Trial* and Scholnick, "Lawsuit Drama."

and strings them together, one finds a compelling argument against apparent divine injustice in which Iyov progresses from complaint to protest and accusation, to considering and then instigating a lawsuit against God. The transition is gradual and develops as the dispute with his friends intensifies. In the book's climactic court scene, Iyov forces God's appearance by means of a series of legally binding oaths, resulting in the appearance of the defendant—God—and Iyov's theophany, which leads to Iyov's retracting his lawsuit, and last but not least to the divine verdict. The law-court motif is used first to debate contemporary theodicies and then to offer a new understanding of the meaning of suffering both for Iyov and the Jewish exiles (of all generations) who heard or read his eponymous book.

As Iyov begins to lament his plight, his friends break their silence too and, in the first cycle, they attempt both comfort and theodicy, to rationalize Iyov's suffering as it relates to divine providence. They offer Iyov the dominant theodicy of the day, according to which suffering comes as a result of sin. It is divine punishment, but even more importantly, it is divine correction. Each friend expounds this theme in turn. Echoing Mishlei (Proverbs) 3:11–12, Eliphaz, for example, declares: "See how happy is the man whom God reproves; / Do not reject the discipline of the Almighty."[6] According to his friends, since Iyov is suffering, he must have sinned and he should be thankful for the wake-up call to mend his ways. He should search out his misdeeds, repent, and return to the correct path; then God will restore him and his fortunes. Of this, they are certain[7] and Iyov himself is honest enough to admit that he too would previously have responded just as his friends do now.[8]

As the dispute continues, the friends' increasingly strident and dogmatic views lead Iyov to respond ever more vehemently in opposing their views and asserting his own innocence. Gradually the dispute shifts focus to one between Iyov and God, in which Iyov is the plaintiff and God is both the defendant from whom Iyov demands an accounting[9] and also the judge to whom Iyov is appealing for justice.[10] After first contemplating litigation in chapter 9, Iyov makes the momentous decision in chapter 13 to actually challenge God legally. At issue are both Iyov's innocence and the justice of

---

6. Iyov 5:17.

7. Eliphaz, Iyov 5:19–27; Bildad, Iyov 8:20–22; Tzophar, Iyov 11:13–20.

8. Iyov 16:2–4

9. See Iyov 9:14–19, 32–35; 13:3, 15–28; 24:1; 31:35–37.

10. See Iyov 9:32–35; 10:2; 13:13–19; 16:18–22; 19:23–29; 27:1–6; 31:35–37.

the divine judgment against him, which has taken the form of suffering. He declares:

> Keep quiet; I will have my say,
> Come what may upon me . . .
> I will take my life in my hands . . .
> Yet I will argue my case before him.
> In this too is my salvation:
> That no impious man can come into his presence.[11]

Iyov is keenly aware of the mortal danger he faces in taking God to court but, so certain is he of his innocence (13:16, 18), he also knows that he can face down his accuser. All he asks is that God not attack or intimidate him (13:20–21) so that the two of them can present their perspectives (13:22–23) more or less as equals.

In chapter 16, Iyov accuses God of persecuting him (16:7–17) yet also looks to God as the Supreme Arbiter to judge the case on the basis of justice (16:18–21). Chapter 19 has Iyov again accusing God of violence and his erstwhile friends of siding with God rather than him (19:13–22). Two chapters later, after more provocation by his friends, Iyov has gotten to the point where he repudiates the very concept of divine justice, noting how the wicked prosper yet mock God. He wonders why they do not receive the punishment they deserve.

Iyov's renunciation of the dominant theodicy of the day provokes Eliphaz to call him a transgressor (22:5–11). Chapters 23–27 represent the pivotal point in the progression of Iyov's speeches as Iyov turns from disputing with his friends to challenging God directly. In chapter 23, Iyov asks God to make known the legal basis for his ill treatment: "If we could meet and have our case," says Iyov, "I would be vindicated—but God does what God wants." In chapter 24, returning to an earlier theme, Iyov again asserts that evildoers do all kinds of misdeeds for which God ought to punish them but instead makes them feel secure. By chapter 27, Iyov does not bother any more to answer his friends' accusations. Instead, he now turns to accuse God. Iyov takes his first oath regarding his integrity and puts his life on the line in so doing:

> By God who has deprived me of justice!
> By *Shaddai* who has embittered my life!

11. Iyov 13:13–16.

> As long as there is life in me,
>
> And God's breath in my nostrils,
>
> My lips will speak no wrong,
>
> Nor my tongue utter deceit.
>
> Far be it from me to say you are right;
>
> Until I die I will maintain my integrity.
>
> I persist in my righteousness and will not yield;
>
> I shall be free of reproach as long as I live.[12]

The oath of innocence concludes Iyov's disputation with his friends.

III IYOV TAKES GOD TO COURT

Iyov now behaves as if a court were in session and he opens his public testimony with a paean to wisdom, concluding that its source is divine.[13] In chapters 29–30, Iyov contrasts the good old days and all his righteousness with his current plight.[14] Iyov's prosecution of God moves toward its climax. Having presented the facts of the case, Iyov concludes his argument with a series of challenges and oaths in chapter 31,[15] such as this one:

> Have I walked with worthless men,
>
> Or my feet hurried to deceit?
>
> Let him weigh me on the scale of righteousness;
>
> Let God ascertain my integrity.
>
> If my feet have strayed from their course,

---

12. Iyov 27:2–6.

13. Chapter 28 is sometimes seen as an insert, a "Hymn to Wisdom," but the words can just as easily come from Iyov's mouth, especially given all the presumed "wisdom" he has heard from his friends. Again foreshadowing God's speeches, the poem asserts that true wisdom is hidden and hard to acquire. In the end, God alone has wisdom and human beings therefore should only stand in awe of God (fear God) and shun evil (which Iyov has always done and which God also acknowledged in 1:8 and 2:3). The conclusion of chapter 28 is remarkably similar to the concluding advice of Kohelet (Ecclesiastes): "Revere (fear) God and observe his commandments" (Koh/Eccl 12:14). For more on the similarity between the two most skeptical books in the Tanakh, see Leo Baeck, "Job and Kohelet: Books of Wisdom," in Glatzer, *Dimensions of Job*, 51–56.

14. In the law-court pattern of prayer, an essential component of the case is to tell the court (God as Judge) about the unjust situation by contrasting the good days of the past with the misery one now endures. This is what Iyov is doing here.

15. Iyov 31:1–4, 5–8, 9–10, 13–17, 19–21, 24–28, 29–34, 38–40.

My heart followed after my eyes,

And a stain sullied my hands,

May I sow, but another reap,

May the growth of my field be uprooted![16]

One must realize the extreme gravity of uttering oaths such as these in biblical times. Although oath-taking was a common practice in ancient Yisrael, full oaths—that is, oaths in which the consequences of swearing falsely are spelled out—are found only twice in the Tanakh.[17] According to *Vayikra* (Leviticus) 5:1, if one hears a public imprecation regarding the withholding of testimony and does not step forward with his information, he is guilty and must atone by making a sin offering.[18] Shemot (Exodus) 22:10 declares that in a disputed matter "an oath before the Lord shall decide between the two of them" who was telling the truth. The use of the oath by Iyov seems meant both to clear Iyov's name and to compel God's testimony.[19]

The rhetorical questions, assertions of innocence, and series of oaths culminate in verses 35–40, in which Iyov pleads for arbitration:

O that I had someone to give me a hearing;

O that *Shaddai* would reply to my writ,

Or my accuser draw up a true bill![20]

16. Iyov 31:5–8.

17. Teh/Pss 7 and 137. Oaths and vows were allowed in the Torah (Dvar/Deut 10:20) and legal steps regarding their use are outlined in Bam/Num 30. The law concerning a suspected adulteress includes both adjuration and ordeal (Bam/Num 5:16ff). Later examples of oath-taking include: Shof/Judg 21:1; 1 Shm/Sam 14:28; 17:55; 20:3; 2 Shm/ Sam 14:19; 1 Mel/Kgs 17:1; and 2 Mel/Kgs 2:2. Swearing by God was seen as adhering to God—see, for example, Teh/Ps 63:12; Yesh/Isa 48:1—and God also joins the people in taking oaths on his name (Yer/Jer 44:26).

18. Other examples of the oath of adjuration are Shof/Judg 17:1–3; 1 Mel/Kgs 8:31–32; and Mish/Prov 29:24.

19. For more on the role of oaths, see Hartley, "From Lament to Oath," 87–88. According to him, whenever there was insufficient evidence for a court to render a decision, or when a claim could not be proven by the plaintiff, a court normally compelled the defendant to take an oath of innocence.

Newsom, *Book of Job*, 185, takes issue with the legal structure and says that Job's final speech is one of testimony, but not in a legal sense, rather simply giving an account of events. However, recitation of the facts of the case in the law-court pattern of prayer is an essential component of building one's case. She does note, correctly I think, that the oaths affirm Iyov's character and the bond of values he shares with his audience while it builds his case against God.

20. Iyov 31:35–37.

Iyov concludes by challenging God to respond with one final full oath, which calls for the very earth to testify to his righteousness. If Iyov is wrong, then the earth, source of blessings, will in effect be cursed and produce naught for him:

> If my land cries out against me,
> Its furrows weep together;
> If I have eaten its produce without payment
> And made its [rightful] owners despair,
> May nettles grow there instead of wheat;
> Instead of barley, stinkweed![21]

If Iyov did not truly believe in divine justice he would not have been so vociferous in seeking his day in court. Furthermore, although the oath was the boldest means a person in ancient Yisrael had to defend a claim of innocence, its use was dependent on a predictable world in which God, contrary to Iyov's accusations, actually intervened based on the truthfulness of the oath taken. The use of oaths has the same expectations of God that the friends and Iyov share: that God will intervene and follow justice. Like "If the glove fits, you must acquit," so too "If the oaths ring true, then Iyov is too." If Iyov had perjured himself, then the oaths would be visited upon him as punishments and his friends would be proved right in their statements about God and suffering. But if Iyov were innocent, then the fact that the consequences of the oaths were averted would prove it.

The use of the law-court here is no mere motif (even if the story itself is mythic). According to the actual use of oaths in a law-court, which forms the basis of Iyov's oath/summons, God *must* appear so that Iyov can confront his accuser and be vindicated. And this is precisely what happens next—or at least should have.

IV ELIHU INTERRUPTS THE PROCEEDINGS

But before God can respond, Elihu pops up as God's self-appointed defense attorney, ready to fill the bill when, in his estimation, Eliphaz, Bildad, and Tsophar have failed (33:5-12). All along, Iyov had wanted a third party to judge/bear witness—earth and heaven (16:19), an umpire (9:33, 16:21), a witness (16:19), an interpreter (16:19, 33:23), a redeemer (19:25), just

---

21. Iyov 31:38-40.

someone (31:35)—even though it is God whom he wishes to confront and God whose justice he seeks. Instead Iyov gets Elihu.

Elihu is a nosy, noisy, and perhaps noisome presence in the book as we have received it, and so, like it or not, his words count. True to his role, Elihu, who thinks so highly of himself that he can have a dialogue all by himself,[22] stakes out a position for his client that is later amplified during the theophany, when God puts in his appearance.

Elihu starts where Iyov leaves off by refuting his claim to innocence and his charge that God does not care (33:8–12a). Instead, Elihu asserts that God communicates in various ways in order to redirect a person's behavior (33:14–16). Sometimes, he says, suffering is a form of preventive discipline (33:16–30; 36:8–12; 36:15–16). Linking Iyov with wicked men who deny God's justice (34:2–9, 36–37), Elihu declares that God is the epitome of justice (34:10–12) upon whom all life depends (34:13–14). In other places, he asserts that God operates by retributive justice (34:11, 21–27) and, since God is the "Just Mighty One" (34:17), Iyov should simply acknowledge his guilt, bear his punishment, and sin no more (34:31–32). Iyov fails to realize that God *does* hear the cry of the oppressed (34:28; 35:9,13) and, though his response is obscured by human evil, nonetheless in due time God will act justly to set things right (35:9–16).

Elihu has offered refinements to the friends' sin-and-punishment model of divine justice: Sometimes it is simply corrective; at other times it is preventive. Sometimes retributive justice is immediate; at other times it is delayed. But make no mistake, says Elihu, God is just and in the end justice will prevail in human society as surely as God rules over heaven and earth.[23]

Elihu concludes by rehearsing God's awesome and providential rule as displayed in nature, by which he controls all human endeavor (36:28–33; 37:12–13), and he asserts that Iyov ought not criticize God because God and God's governance are greater than anything he could imagine:

> See, God is beyond reach in his power;
> Who governs like him?
> Who ever reproached him for his conduct?
> Who ever said, "You have done wrong"? . . .

22. See Iyov 32:6–10; 33:3 and 33b; 36:4; and 34:1; 35:1; 36:1 respectively.

23. The best analysis of Elihu's speeches, in my opinion, remains Glatzer, "Knowest Thou," in *Essays in Jewish Thought.* Glatzer draws attention to the underlying theme of true knowledge, a theme that unites Elihu's and God's speeches (and makes one suspect that Elihu is therefore a later insertion).

See, God is greater than we can know;
The number of his years cannot be counted.[24]

Shaddai—we cannot attain to him;
He is great in power and justice
And abundant in righteousness;
He does not torment.
Therefore, men are in awe of him
Whom none of the wise can perceive.[25]

Acting as God's self-appointed defense attorney, Elihu scolds Iyov that because he knows so little it is absurd for him to challenge God's justice (37:14–24) and, besides, God is too lofty to be affected by human behavior (35:5–8) and too powerful to be challenged (34:13–15; 36:22–25).

But Elihu is wrong on all counts. The oaths ultimately have their desired effect of "forcing God's hand" and God shows up to answer Iyov's charges (38:1—40:2; 40:7—41:26). After speaking his mind, Elihu simply vanishes from the story just as suddenly as he had appeared. Then God appears to respond to Iyov directly.

V   GOD PUTS IN AN APPEARANCE

Without Elihu's interruption of the proceedings,[26] God's arrival on the scene would follow immediately after Iyov's taking his oath of innocence, as would a defendant's turn in an actual law-court setting. Iyov's court case has run its course. The book has used the law-court motif to challenge the dominant theodicy of its day, which, in essence, blamed the victim for the suffering endured. The motif now culminates in God's appearance in the story, through which a new understanding of the meaning of suffering is proposed.

God appears, yet Iyov remains intact. He has not been destroyed by his oaths or for his *chutzpah*. Rebuking Iyov for his lack of knowledge but

---

24. Iyov 36:22–26.

25. Iyov 37:23–24.

26. Many scholars consider the speeches of Elihu to be a later insertion. See Gruber, "Elihu the Intruder," in *The Jewish Study Bible*, 1546–47, and Newsom, *Book of Job*, 35, for a summary of their reasons.

challenging him to stand up for himself,[27] God demands: "Will you impugn my justice? Would you condemn me that you may be right?" "Shall one who should be disciplined complain against *Shaddai*? He who arraigns God must respond."[28] As many a reader of Iyov has observed, God never gives Iyov a straight answer to his demand for justice. Although it was appropriate for Iyov to take God to court based on his limited understanding of how he assumed God operates (i.e., with justice), God could have chosen to ignore this puny human power play to force his appearance. But, although God chose to participate, he did not follow court procedure and actually address Iyov's complaint; in fact God chose to ignore it.

Unlike Elihu, who blithely linked social justice with God's control of nature, God (more honestly) declares that there is no justice in Creation, at least not any kind that human beings can comprehend. This totally undermines everything that Iyov and his friends understand about how the world works. Since divine justice is not human justice, God could simply have ignored the summons triggered by Iyov's oath and remained silent and aloof (as Elihu had said God would).

Instead God tries to turn the table on his accuser by overwhelming Iyov with rhetorical questions confirming that God's wisdom and power are far beyond those of mortal human beings (which Iyov already had acknowledged in chapter nine). God's first speech is about cosmic design; the second is about his control and power. God argues that Iyov needs to show he could do a better job running Creation (40:6–14) if he is to stand as God's accuser. God suggests that Iyov's lawsuit is only valid if Iyov can prove his capacity to understand the way the universe is governed.

VI IYOV'S RESPONSE

Iyov had demanded that his accuser appear and God, perhaps surprisingly, has done so. Now Iyov refuses to be baited by God; he does not attempt to answer God's challenge; he simply backs down and retracts his suit (42:6). Iyov realizes that his perception of the divine order was in fact negligible and for this reason his action ultimately was misguided. However, once Iyov acknowledged this, God could later pronounce him to be in the right, at least compared to his friends' point of view. Humbled by *Shaddai*'s

27. Iyov 38:2–3.

28. Iyov 40:8 and 40:2, respectively.

appearance and overwhelmed by the divine deluge of words, Iyov acknowledges God's greater power and decides not to press his case.

Iyov is a changed man as a result of his theophany and he acknowledges this: "I had heard you with my ears, but now I see you with my eyes"[29]—but he never says "I have sinned" or "I am wrong"; he only declares "I am of small worth." Although Iyov retreats into silence (40:3–5), it is not the silence of submission. Noting that the word ידעתי in the written text of verse 42:2 is different from the vocalized text as designated by the Masorite scribes, Jonathan Schraub points out that while the vocalized version is pietistic and submissive, "*I know* [*yada'ati* ידעתי] you can do all these things," the actual written text is defiant: "*You know* [*yada'ata* ידעת] you can do all these things."[30]

God's plan is unlimited and incomprehensible to human beings. It is *nifla'ot* (wondrous beyond comprehension). So, although Iyov is none the wiser about why bad things happen to basically good people, he now has had a divine revelation, a direct experience with the Creator.[31] Even if Iyov never receives a direct answer to his challenge of why the innocent suffer, the theophany has made it clear that God is neither as inattentive nor as remote as Iyov had charged.[32]

Unfortunately, one cannot state definitively how Iyov felt because the exact meaning of the idiosyncratic Hebrew idiom used in these verses in particular is clouded. Many scholars note the problem of translating Hebrew word *emas* אמאס and *v'nihamtee* ונחמתי, based on the roots *m's* מס and *nhm* נחם, respectively, in 42:6. *m's* can mean to loathe, recant, dissolve/melt, or despise but here it lacks a direct object,[33] so we don't know of what

29. Iyov 42:5

30. Both readings remain legitimate in Jewish tradition. See Schraub, "For the Sin," 439–42. Miles, *God*, 317, likewise sees Iyov's two final responses as defiant. Habel, *Book of Job*, 578, sees Iyov's final job speech as tongue-in-cheek. Iyov confesses guilt even though innocent and God accepts his confession. His speech is his final act of defiance. Iyov admits to limits to his knowledge but he rejects a deity who overwhelms a despairing human being. When Iyov says "he sees," Habel interprets this to mean that Iyov sees God as unjust, unfeeling, and cruel—a most unique reading but plausible nonetheless.

31. Iyov 42:5. Wolde, "Job 42, 1–6," 242, accurately notes that "The words from the whirlwind have profoundly transformed Job's orientation on YHWH and the world."

32. A significant question: Were his friends privy to this whirlwind experience too—after all, God does address Eliphaz subsequently—or was Iyov's experience private and internal? Iyov's vindication depends on God's confirming Iyov publicly in some way, whether in a shared theophany, the shared rebuke, or both.

33. In every other case in the Tanakh where the first person singular imperfect of *m's*

Iyov recants or despises. Some translations[34] render it "I abhor myself" even though the verb *m's* is not in a reflexive form. The next verb, *nhm*, is also disputed. *Nhm* is usually combined with the preposition *al* על to mean "concerning," and it connotes a change of mind. But here *nhm* is often understood as if it were using the preposition *beh* ב, meaning "in." So the text could be rendered "I repent/relent *of* dust and ashes" or it could mean "I repent/relent *in* dust and ashes" or it could understood as "I repent/relent *being but* dust and ashes." Is Iyov forsaking his position of lamentation and returning to normal life from his place of humiliation, or is he affecting a stance of repentance and submission as traditionally interpreted?[35]

Jonathan Schraub points out that the two verbs *emas* and *v'nihamtee* "are poetic *hendiadys* . . . intended to be read together" but "virtually every biblical translation ignores the crucial poetic structure and wedges a presumed object between the two verbs." He notes that the "impossibility of arriving at a single consensus reading . . . does not justify the wholesale revision of the sense of the verse by interpolating non-existent words and ignoring established poetic structure to serve the ulterior purposes of institutionalized religious notions of piety."[36]

Scholarly disagreement notwithstanding, I think it likely that by declaring "something" with regards to "dust and ashes," Iyov was acknowledging his human limitations and humility before God much as Avraham had done. In fact, both Avraham and Iyov use the same term, "dust and ashes," precisely when challenging God to be more just. Humility and *chutzpah* appear to go together hand in hand, as well they should when a mortal creature confronts *El Shaddai*, Creator of all. Noting this parallel usage, I would suggest that when Iyov "recants and relents,"[37] he acknowledges and regrets his challenging God as a mere creature of "dust and ashes," an

---

is used it is followed by an object. See Mandelkern, *Concordantiae Hebraicae*, 656.

34. The Jerusalem Bible for one, based on British translations.

35. For the Rambam (Maimonides), "repent of dust and ashes" meant Iyov was leaving his place of mourning and lamenting for those things to which he formerly was so attached. See Maimonides, *Guide of the Perplexed*, III.497.

36. Schraub, "For the Sins," 447–48 and 460 note 47. Habel, *Book of Job*, 576, states: "If, however, we recognize the legal framework of Job's response, then a clue as to the object of the verb *m's* may be found in 31:13, where Job asserts that he did not "dismiss/reject" the case "of his manservant."

For more on scholarly views, see Schraub, "For the Sins," 443–47; Habel, *Book of Job*, 576–77; Wolde, "Job 42, 1–6," 242–47; and Janzen, *Job*, 255–58.

37. Iyov 40:4–5; 42:2–3, 6.

"earthling" lacking true knowledge of how Creation operates, and he backs off from his lawsuit—but never his claim to innocence.[38]

The text, nonetheless, remains equivocal and so its meaning must remain forever in question, as Mayer Gruber laconically notes:

> As Job's final comment, this verse would seem to be key to understanding the book as a whole . . . Thus, the highly ambiguous poetry concludes with this seemingly simple but ambiguous verse. Whatever it means, the Lord seems to be satisfied that Job has responded adequately (see 40:5), so the poetic section of the work is concluded.[39]

VII THE PERPLEXITIES ADDED BY THE PROLOGUE AND EPILOGUE

Trying to make sense of this ambiguity would be challenging enough, but to do so within the context of the prologue and epilogue, which sandwich the meat of the text we have been analyzing, only adds complexity to the perplexity of Iyov's final statements.

The prologue in heaven casts a unique perspective over all that subsequently transpires and, at least for me, makes the intent of the redactor(s) uncertain. Because of the prologue, we know what God and *HaSattan* know; without it, we enter into the world of mere mortals, knowing only what they know or think they know. But, even though we enter into their world and listen in on their debate, we also retain in the back of our minds the heavenly knowledge that Iyov is truly innocent and it is all just a test, a friendly little wager between two divine beings.

But is the view of the prologue meant to take precedence over what follows? If so, then two things are made clear from the start (and which many a reader may subsequently forget while listening to Iyov and his friends argue). First, we immediately must reject the Deuteronomic explanation

---

38. Given how much scholars have wrangled over the precise meaning of Iyov's final words, one has to wonder how those people who simply heard them being read aloud might have understood them. It demonstrates our preoccupation with the written word down through many centuries at the expense of the oral/aural tradition.

39. Gruber, "Introduction" in *The Jewish Study Bible*, 1561, under the heading "Job's Recantation." See also Wolde, "Job 42, 1–6," 238, on the ambiguity of these verses and theme of "knowing." Westermann, *Structure*, 128, points out that Iyov's knowing is like a salvation oracle in Teh/Pss 20:7, 56:10; 140:13; and 135:5–6.

for suffering—that suffering comes as a result of sin—since we know from the beginning of the story that Iyov is innocent and God's actions (in this case) are arbitrary and unfair. Second, and consequently, the Deuteronomic explanation itself is invalidated because we, the readers, know that God and *HaSattan* are solely responsible for Iyov's misery; Iyov's behavior did not trigger retributive justice. The prologue makes it apparent that there is no divine order, only divine whim. This appears to Iyov as random (mis-)fortune, which, whether for good or evil, he nonetheless—and correctly from a monotheistic perspective—views as coming from God.[40]

Iyov, for all his kvetching, is still attached to the concept of divine justice because he believes that an innocent man like himself should not suffer. Like Avraham,[41] Iyov expects God to follow this moral order, an order that should be humanly understandable and is applicable to all, even God. Yet, by the end of the book, the concept of retributive justice has been repudiated three times: by the message of the prologue, by the experience of Iyov himself, and by God's own words.

And, just as the prologue subverts the intense disputation that follows, so too the epilogue undermines all that precedes it. God has just finished describing a world that operates without the system of retributive justice. God lauds himself, not as the God of history, but as the Creator who maintains a delicate balance between chaos and order in nature. Our human sense of justice and order does not apply to God or Creation. However, in the epilogue, Iyov's piety leads precisely to a restoration of his prosperity, thereby confirming the justice inherent in the Deuteronomic system.[42] In an ironic (and possibly playful) twist, God actually follows the commandment concerning a thief making restitution by doubling Iyov's former possessions, which had been unjustly taken from him.[43] The point is that after declaring that all the rules don't apply, God follows the rules and does exactly what is expected by people of their deity—to behave justly and mercifully.

Iyov's vindication depends on God's confirming Iyov's innocence publicly in some way and this also occurs in the epilogue. God tells Iyov's fickle friends via Eliphaz, "I am incensed at you . . . for you have not spoken the

40. Iyov 1:21 and 2:10.

41. Ber/Gen 18:25.

42. See Clines, "Why Is There a Book of Job," 18.

43. Shem/Exod 22:3, 6. But God doesn't give Iyov double the number of children because they are a divine gift to begin with.

truth about me as did my servant Iyov," and orders them to offer sacrifices and ask Iyov to intercede on their behalf" (42:7–9). In God's eyes, the issue is how to talk about God, and clearly God is saying that the friends are wrong in their views. But in what way is Iyov correct?

What is the truth Iyov spoke to which God refers? Is it in Iyov's acknowledgment of his "dust and ashes" state of being, like Avraham did? Or is it in his fiery backhanded affirmations of his expectation of divine justice (even though God has said our human sense of justice doesn't apply to Creation)? One key distinction to note: Iyov speaks directly *to* God whereas his friends only speak *about* God. Is this what God approves of? (And if so, what does this say about theologians?) Although God tells the friends Iyov spoke the truth, did God do so in Iyov's presence so that Iyov also heard this important vindication? Or maybe Iyov just knew he was speaking truth to power all along and didn't need this confirmation.[44] Perhaps even though Iyov was wrong to think that God could be bound by human conceptions of justice, God appreciated Iyov's honest juxtaposition of his life experience with his belief system and his angry assertion that he was, in heart and deed, a basically good man. Perhaps God also was expressing a preference for being held to that supra-divine standard of justice that Avraham and Iyov articulate rather than the traditional and more theologically correct words that the friends had uttered—even though *all these* are human conceptions inadequate to the task of representing God's ways.

In the end, we are left with pieces of a puzzle that don't quite fit together. Perhaps the redactor(s) wanted to complicate an already complex dialogue by adding a "higher" level of understanding from the get-go and muddling things up at the end? Or perhaps they simply wanted to include all components of the story that they had in their possession? Taken as a whole—which *is* the way the book of Iyov has come down to us—the prologue and epilogue together with the dialogues that take up most of the book remain a challenge for generations of readers to chew on and have

44. Some additional questions about the epilogue: Does having new children really compensate for the dead ones? Is it simply a matter of numerical restitution? How did Iyov feel? And what about Mrs. Iyov—how much suffering did she have to endure to bear another twelve children?! And what happened to Elihu, he who spoke so confidently about God? Did he slink off during or after the theophany? Also, one has to wonder why there is no epilogue conversation in heaven between God and *HaSattan*. Was it simply that his job was done once Iyov passed his test and *HaSattan* was off investigating other individuals while God had other concerns to attend to? Or perhaps there was a concluding conversation between the two of them off stage—but God alone knows the content of that!

provided fodder for countless scholars. Bruce Zuckerman sums up the problem succinctly:

> The book of Job therefore appears to be at odds with itself and however one may attempt to resolve its contradictory picture, the result never seems to be quite successful. Like oil and water, the Prose Frame Story and the Poem naturally tend to disengage from one another despite all efforts to homogenize them.[45]

Given all this intentional or unintentional ambiguity, what is the meaning of the book as a whole? To answer this question, we need to examine the role of the audience and the historical context of the book of Iyov.

VIII IYOV'S THEOPHANY IS THE PEOPLE'S THEOPHANY

In the poetic section of the book, the listeners/readers initially are like Elihu, sitting silently observing the escalating dispute between Iyov and his friends. However, by the time Iyov makes his series of oaths, he is acting as if a court were in session. But who constitutes this court? In Elihu's speeches, specifically in chapter 34, it seems as though he is speaking to more people than Iyov and his friends (34:2–4, 10a, 16, 34–35) and some of his rhetorical flourishes seem to indicate the same. One scholar suggests it is a "super addressee," i.e., in front of an assembly of some sort, but it is also taking place before us, the reader/listeners.[46] With Elihu's departure, we, the listeners/ readers, become witnesses to the lawsuit between Iyov and God—perhaps even a jury of sorts to deliberate the merits of the case after the fact. What a responsibility—and if that is so for us moderns, how much the more so for the book's ancient listeners/readers!

I think it is difficult for modern people to appreciate the impact this part of the story might have had in times past. For one thing, Iyov often was believed to have been a real person and not a mythic character.[47] For another, given what we know about the use of oaths in ancient Israel and well beyond that time, it must have been terrifying to hear these oaths invoked

---

45. Zuckerman, *Job the Silent*, 14.

46. Newsom, *Book of Job*, 186.

47. See the discussion by the rabbis in *b. Bava Batra* 14b–15b on whether Iyov was a real person and when he lived, or his story is a parable; also on whether or not he was a Jew or a heathen.

because oaths were literal and causative, not figurative or symbolic.[48] And when God appears after being called to accounts, it is *El Shaddai* in the flesh, so to speak, confronting not only Iyov, a real man, but by extension all the listeners/readers who form this court. In other words, to the listeners/readers of yore, Iyov was a real person who, unlike most people, actually took God to court and for whom God actually appeared to answer his charges! Since they served *in situ* as that court, Iyov's theophany thus became their theophany as well. This must have been an electrifying moment.[49]

The core of the book of Iyov presents the dominant theodicy that was current among the Jewish exiles in Babylon and later, with which the people had to grapple. The Jews of the First Exile needed to rationalize God's apparent anger that had allowed for the Babylonian conquest, the destruction of the First Temple, and the Exile.[50] Like Iyov, the exiles were confronted from both within and without by voices offering the same tired and untrue words as those of Iyov's friends, who preached that bad things only happen to people who deserve them. Iyov's friends all present variations on the Deuteronomic rationale for suffering: Since God is just, and suffering only comes to those who have sinned, therefore Iyov/the people must be guilty of having sinned. Just as Iyov was called upon to acknowledge his sins, so too exilic Jews were urged to find the collective sin(s) that had precipitated the divine punishment.

But some people, like Iyov, also had angry words for those who castigated them, who claimed to know the mind of God and the meaning of suffering. Like Iyov, these people knew that they were basically innocent—that is, they may have sinned, but their punishment outweighed the alleged crimes. And, just as Iyov was pushed via the dispute with his friends

48. In the law concerning a suspected adulteress (Bam/Num 5:11–31), for example, the adjuration concludes with an ordeal that was expected to show guilt or innocence. Iyov's oath was expected to have the same result: if they came to pass, he was guilty; if not, he was innocent; and if God failed to appear to answer Iyov's complaint, then, too, Iyov was innocent.

49. Over the centuries, those fortunate few who had the time and ability to read and study also had an opportunity to reflect on the totality of the book with all its ambiguities, intentional or otherwise, pouring over the text word by word, letter by letter. Examined this way, the theophany is related rather than experienced as it is when heard read aloud. This takes the book's impact down a few notches as the reader/student is given the opportunity to be a reflector. Most moderns fall into the category of reflectors since we tend to read the book (as opposed to listening and understanding as the book is read aloud), and we read it symbolically at that.

50. This idea is developed further in Laytner, *Arguing with God*, 20–22, 28–32, 34–38.

into a position of asserting that God is unjust, so too, among some of the exiles, the Deuteronomic explanation was rejected in favor of individual accountability and a challenging of divine justice.[51] Lastly, like Iyov, they yearned for a day of vindication, heralded by the appearance of their God, who would acknowledge their innocence and restore them to all that had been theirs before.

Both the prologue and the epilogue portray God as the source of all, both the apparently good and the perceived evil (sometimes translated as "misfortune")—God alone and none other.[52] The idea of an all-encompassing monotheism is a radical concept developed in other postexilic works,[53] probably as a result of the Jewish encounter with the Zoroastrian religion.[54] This may be discomfiting to some contemporary ears, but as Iyov acknowledges—and as God's speech intimates—good and evil both are part of the divine order that exists in Creation, although that order is beyond our comprehension and outside of our human explanatory framework. God implies that there may be imperfection in Creation but challenges the listener/reader: "Who can do a better job?"

In Elihu's speeches and the theophany, the book offers the ancient listener/reader an additional message. According to Elihu, the appropriate attitude regarding suffering—strongly reinforced by the theophany and epilogue—is one of humble submission to God's apparent will with the

51. See Eicha/Lam 3 and Laytner, *Arguing with God*, 28–32.

52. Iyov 2:10; 42:11. Similarly, see the famous passage Yesh/Isa 45:7, thought by historical-critical biblical scholars to have been composed during or after the Exile: "I am YHVH, there is none else. I form light and create darkness. I make good fortune and create calamity—I, YHVH, do all these things." For a modern application of this monotheistic principle, see Schraub, "For the Sins," 448–49, who briefly discusses Carl Jung's *Answer to Job*.

53. See also Eicha/Lam 3:38 and Yesh/Isa 42:18–25; 44:6–8; 45:5–8, 18–23.

54. As the Jewish religion was being reconstructed after the catastrophe of the First Exile, these Zoroastrian teachings began to filter into the Jewish religious culture. See Zaehner, *Comparison of Religions*, 134–53, and Mary Boyce, *Zoroastrianism*. James Barr, in "The Question of Religious Influence," critiques this connection for lack of solid evidence, even though he notes that it is conceivable that ideas were absorbed directly in Persia or indirectly via Jewish contact with Hellenistic Greek mediators of Persian thought. The problem is that it is hard to document what took place in the early stages of post–First Temple Judaism. Most likely transmission primarily occurred organically, through private dialogues and social engagement rather than through books and formal religious interactions. For a fuller discussion, see the prolegomena in Silverman, *Persepolis and Jerusalem*.

emunah (trust/faith/belief) that all will eventually be well since it is part of God's inscrutable plan.

In the end, the life lesson offered by the book is this: Human beings should stand in awe of God (fear God) and shun evil, as Iyov declared: "See! Awe [fear] of *YHVH* is wisdom; / To shun evil is understanding."[55] One must continue to serve God (in the Jewish parlance, follow the *mitzvot*) not only in spite of all adversity, but also without the expectation of an explanation or even the expectation of understanding. Thus, regardless of the confusing subtleties of the book's message, the ancient audience could also take away a message of comfort: The hope that in due time they would be vindicated by divine justice and restored, just as Iyov had been.[56] Later generations of Jews would continue to partake of this hope in an ever more messianic way.

IX   AND THE MEANING IS . . . THEOPHANY TRUMPS THEODICY

The book of Iyov has presented a number of theodicies for the listener/reader to consider. The prologue clearly states that suffering is but a heavenly test of a good man, which the friends then see as divine punishment for some unnamed sin(s) on Iyov's part. The proper and normative response to the prologue's theodicy, which Iyov attempts, is to endure everything in faith and trust in God; the proper and normative response to the dialogue's theodicy, which Iyov comes to reject categorically, is to repent and return to the right path. Elihu, perhaps representing a later generation's perspective (that of the youth), offers refinements of the friends' perspective, advancing

55. Iyov 28:28. Iyov's words here are remarkably similar to two other "wisdom" books: Mishlei (Proverbs) and Kohelet (Ecclesiastes). Mish/Prov 3:7–8 is almost a summary for the book of Iyov: "Do not be wise in your own eyes; be in awe of (fear) YHVH and shun evil. It will be a cure for your body, a tonic for your bones," while *Kohelet* concludes: "Revere (fear) God and observe his commandments" (Koh/Eccl 12:14).

56. See a summary of this new emerging theodicy in Laytner, *Arguing with God*, 36–38. Kepnes, "Job and Post-Holocaust Theodicy," sees in the epilogue a messianic hope of restoration. He also believes that the book of Iyov offers a "rent" theology, a theology of contradiction, for although Iyov knows he cannot win his suit nonetheless he insists on pursuing it thereby showing that he never gives up on God and God's justice. He continues to believe in justice in spite of an unjust God and he continues to believe in God in spite of his belief in justice. This line of theology has been developed in many of Elie Wiesel's works. See Laytner's analysis of Wiesel in *Arguing with God*, 214–27. See also Schraub, "For the Sins," 451, 454–55.

the idea that sometimes suffering comes as a divine warning and is meant to be preventative. He also opines that God's justice, which fills all Creation, including human society and individual lives, operates on its own schedule, not ours—but it does happen.

God's words confirm only part of Elihu's statements and offer yet a fourth perspective. Yes, God's providential wisdom fills all Creation, including the human condition, but there is no mention that this divine wisdom includes justice as we humans understand it.[57] Accepting that the one God is the source of all and that God's operation of things is beyond human understanding was the beginning of Iyov's awareness of the greater reality beyond his personal situation.[58] The two were simply not linked in the way he and his friends had assumed them to be. God did not deign to explain the providential workings of the universe to a mere mortal, but the theophany itself provided Iyov with an awareness of the grand scope of divine providence, and his having been answered brought him some sense of enlightenment and at least a certain degree of inner peace.[59]

Iyov's response, coupled with God's remarks to Eliphaz in the epilogue, suggest that the proper response to suffering is: first, to accept that we cannot fathom a rationale for it; second, we can protest about the injustice of it all if necessary; and third, let go and move on. In the end, the book of Iyov proposes not theology or philosophy, but an experience, a concrete sense of connection with God, as the answer to the problem of suffering. Ironically, Iyov started off with the right attitude until the words of his wife and friends knocked him off center. Then it took a divine revelation to restore his equilibrium. Granted, this experience is not bestowed on everyone in need, but through Iyov's example we learn that our suffering is somehow

57. Tsevat, "Meaning of the Book of Job," 90, has suggested that the message of Job is that God is neither a just God nor an unjust God, simply God.

58. The theme of God's grandeur and the inability of human beings to know God's plan in its entirety is also taken up by other post-exilic works: Eicha/Lam 3:37–39; Yeh/Ezek 18:2, 29; Yesh/Isa 40:12–31; 42:18–25; 45:9–13; 55:8–9.

59. Although it is clear that in the biblical book the restoration of Iyov's fortunes was meant to be a consolation, later Jewish scholars noted that nowhere in the book of Iyov is there a suggestion of recompense in the World to Come. Iyov in fact appears to deny it in 7:9: "So whoever goes down to She'ol does not come up." The reason for this, of course, is that the concept of the World to Come hadn't yet arrived. It is a later rabbinic concept and it would have done much to solve Iyov's dilemma had he known about it: Iyov would have understood he was just being tested with "sufferings of love," and once he had demonstrated that he really was serving God disinterestedly, his undeserved sufferings in this life would have been compensated for in the World to Come.

part of the scheme of things and that suffering does not have to mean feeling a sense of isolation from God.

The book teaches that the Deuteronomic doctrine of the causal connection between suffering and moral evil is untenable (although many people, both Jewish and non-Jewish, continue to adhere to it even to this day); that Creation is evidence of God's providential wisdom—but not necessarily of divine justice as we conceive it; that the role of justice in the human condition is something that God chooses not to address; and that it is acceptable to challenge God regarding perceived injustice but, because it is humanly impossible to understand the totality of divine providence, protest is ultimately irrelevant, even if it is spiritually and emotionally therapeutic. This is a radical new theodicy and who better than God to deliver it to the people via the theophany to Iyov?

The law-court motif, which is based on the theological assumption that there is a just order to Creation to which even God is subordinate, enabled Iyov first to question his fate in general terms, then gradually to turn this into a legal pleading of his case, and finally to confront God through a series of legally binding oaths. Although God appears to answer Iyov's charges, the logic of the law-court motif is ultimately undone by the theophany, in which God asserts that whatever order pervades Creation is incomprehensible to humankind. Revelation has trumped human reason. A divine order is affirmed in the theophany yet also undone by it, since we simply lack the necessary knowledge to discuss divine providence—a not unreasonable conclusion for a faith that has revelation at its core. Centuries later, Rabbi Yannai summarized the rabbinic message of the book of Iyov well for future generations, declaring: "It is beyond our power to understand why the wicked are at ease or why the righteous suffer"[60]—not that this ever prevented anyone from speculating.[61]

---

60. *Pirkei Avot* 4:19.

61. For some summaries of how Iyov has been interpreted through the ages, see Glatzer, *Dimensions of Job*, 12–34; Crenshaw, *Reading Job*, 25–40; Burrell, *Deconstructing Theodicy*, 83–105; and Joel Allen, "Job 3."

Chapter 2

The Prologue
In Which Our Family Is Afflicted

YHVH [the LORD[1]] replied to *HaSattan* [the Adversary], "See, all that he has is in your power; only do not lay a hand on him."
(Iyov 1:12)

IN THE SPRING OF 1999, my wife's brother, a man in his mid-sixties, died rather suddenly of bone cancer. On my family's side, I lost an aunt in the summer and an uncle in the fall. That same autumn, my wife Merrily, then in her mid-fifties, was diagnosed with ovarian cancer and then, two days later, her sister was diagnosed with an inoperable brain tumor. My wife had surgery and then spent the next six months in chemotherapy; her sister died within six weeks, sliding out of this world as she slipped deeper into sleep. She was sixty-three years of age.

The day we buried my sister-in-law, my mother, back in my hometown of Toronto, was admitted to a hospital suffering from heart failure. With the help of a pacemaker she recovered, but four days before the year's end my father dropped dead, felled by a massive heart attack. To say that we were reeling from shock is an understatement. And then, just to make sure I truly comprehended my Iyov-like situation, I slipped on some ice, deeply

1. YHVH is the ineffable name of the Jewish God, often rendered into English by scholars as "Yahweh", but spoken in Hebrew as *Adonai*, meaning "Lord."

bruising my lower back, and just as I was able to stand again I got a bad case of shingles at the same latitude.

In early 2000, I was given a three-month sabbatical following my wife's completion of her chemo treatment and her return to health. The plan was that we would travel to Paris, where we would celebrate her escape from cancer by enjoying the sites and, coincidently, I would work on a book on the meaning of suffering. Instead, life intervened. Our eldest daughter, Amy, at the time a vital and vibrant thirty-year-old woman with a one-and-a-half-year old son and a husband, was diagnosed with acute myelogenous leukemia. She spent the next three months receiving and then recuperating from intensive chemotherapy, including an entire month in the hospital. We "inherited" a very distraught and confused little grandson, who came to live with us, and still later our daughter and her husband joined their son at our house for several months.

But while Amy was receiving chemotherapy, I had to rush to Toronto for nearly three weeks while my mother lay in the intensive care unit, dearly tempted to join her husband in the Great Beyond. That was a scene repeated a number of times in the years ahead, including a long hospital stay following a heart valve replacement.

In December of 2000, my wife had emergency surgery for abdominal adhesions caused by her previous surgery for her cancer. The operation took place on the first anniversary of my dad's death (a major date in the Jewish mourning process), with our daughter in another hospital being treated again for her leukemia. I remember shuttling back and forth between hospitals, between daughter and wife, still grieving for my father, torn in more ways than imaginable.

Unfortunately, following the surgery, my wife's incision became infected and she spent a month more in the hospital, then three months laid up at home, while she healed from the inside out and I cleaned and dressed her foot-long wound on a daily basis. But ever so slowly she did recover.

For a while life seemed to return to almost normal as our daughter continued her chemo for the next year and then went into remission. When my mother-in-law died in July 2001, at the fairly decent old age of ninety-two, we began to hope that our lives were again on a more expected course for the first time in over two years. However, just two months later, our daughter's cancer returned and we realized that this was not to be. (Cynically, I "thanked" God for having allowed our daughter to go into remission so that we could focus on my mother-in-law's dying for a couple of months.

Only God could have known that we could not have handled both crises simultaneously.)

In the spring of 2002, after more chemo had failed to bring our daughter's leukemia under control, Amy underwent a successful stem cell transplant. For the next two years we celebrated and hoped, rejoiced when she became pregnant with her second child, and held our breath as the heralded two-year point approached. But, like a marathon runner whose body gives out within sight of the finish line, Amy's leukemia hit her again just days before the anxiously anticipated anniversary in the spring of 2004. More chemo followed, which her fetus shared, and then ultimately she endured another stem cell transplant after her baby was born prematurely. But by the summer of 2005 it was clear to even the most hope-deluded of us that there was nothing anyone could do to prevent her body's demise. We brought Amy to our house for her last few weeks so that her boys could have a refuge in their own home and Amy could have care, rest, and tranquility in ours. She died and was buried on Labor Day weekend 2005.

Our family was devastated. My wife lost a soulmate, her eldest daughter; my two too-young grandsons lost their mother; my daughters lost a sister; my son-in-law lost his wife and mother of his children; and I lost a stepdaughter with whom, thanks to her children, I was finally able to build a good relationship. It was just as if a huge wave and knocked us all over so that we each couldn't differentiate up from down, where the sky was or where to ground our feet. Over and over we tumbled, banging into each other as we struggled for emotional balance. But slowly, over years, our shrunken family gradually found its foothold again; mended our souls as best we could, each one in his or her own way; and trudged on.

When my own mother finally died in July 2007 at the age of eighty-nine from a combination of mini-strokes and esophageal cancer, we believed—and life seemed to bear it out—that the cloud that had hung over our lives had at long last moved on to darken the lives of some other unfortunate souls.

Then, suddenly, three years later, in March 2010, Merrily received a surprise diagnosis of metastasized ovarian cancer starting in her spleen and was given less than a year to live. She followed the usual surgery and chemo routine, but the treatment wasn't working and she suffered so much under chemotherapy that life lost its value. After three rounds of chemo, she left cancer treatment for hospice care and spent the last months of her life feeling better than she had for months prior. But all things must come to an end, and that included her life and our time together. She died on 24 October 2010; she was only sixty-eight.

From her first intuition that the cancer had returned until her final breath, we had nine months. Just like a pregnancy. But where a pregnancy builds new life, cancer destroys it, slowly, inexorably. And even though we knew what was in store, in the end, when death came, it still was a terrible shock. In retrospect, it was as if yet one more huge wave, a tsunami, had come along and swept her and our future together away with one terrible inundation. My hopes and dreams littered the shore like a jumbled mass of flotsam and nothing would ever be the same again.

Loss and grief are deep-seated, gut-felt emotions, and I was awash in my feelings. Although I could—and did—make myself the center of these dramatic events, just as Iyov did too, in fact I was only peripheral to them. I had to remind myself that, although I was grieving deeply, the real tragedy belonged to those in my family who had actually died (like Iyov's unnamed children). My tragedy lay in having witnessed their suffering and deaths. Like Iyov, I had survived all these tragedies and I remained alive to try to make sense of it all in the life after.

Chapter 3

Responding to Iyov's "Friends"
Trying to Make Sense of Suffering

"But you invent lies; / All of you are quacks. / If only you would keep quiet / It would be considered wisdom on your part."
(Iyov 13:4-5)

I   THE RANDOM TERROR IN LIFE

WHEN MY LATE WIFE worked at Seattle's Woodland Park Zoo, I saw more than my share of films about life on the African savannah. One set of images stands out in my mind from these sorts of films: A herd of zebra or other such creatures suddenly erupting in terrified flight as a lion or cheetah charges through the herd to single out one beast for slaughter. Then, once the deed is done, the herd returns to its normal munching. The carnivore is an instrument of random terror in the daily life of the herd.

I associate this image with cars speeding along a highway. Off they go, always exceeding the speed limit, until a hidden state patrol car pounces on the unsuspecting pack. One car is singled out and halted; the rest slow down, take a look, shake their heads, and drive more slowly for a couple of minutes. Then they're off again until the next time. The speed trap is an instrument of random terror for travelers on the highway.

Human life is not much different. We go to work and live our lives, but always with a lurking awareness and a silent dread of disease and death. Then someone we know is brought down by some malady, and we offer our condolences and support, we shake our heads, utter private thanks that it wasn't us, and return to living life as normal until the next time. Disease and death—and the occasional natural catastrophe—are instruments of random terror in our daily lives.

Now the beast does not ask why the big cat chases it as prey, and we all know why a state trooper pulls over a speeding motorist, but, try as we might, we can never fathom the random terror of disease and death.

For generations, humanity has tried to make sense out of suffering; each religion has offered a variety of explanations to comfort those in need. We crave a sense of order as a protection against a world of random chaos, where terror can run amok. Traditionally, God has offered that protection and I think it is human nature, nurtured in us from infancy, to want God to be—and to conceive of God as being—some sort of super-parent, watching over us, protecting us, punishing wrongdoers and rewarding the doers of good. So what happens when evil befalls us?

II GOD IS THE SOURCE OF ALL /
NOT LETTING THE CREATOR OFF THE HOOK

The Abrahamic faiths[1] teach that God is actively involved in history: selecting individuals through whom to reveal his will; intervening in human affairs; testing, punishing, and rewarding individuals and whole nations based on their adherence to divinely revealed moral laws and as part of some divine plan. This traditional belief is called divine providence, according to which God oversees and/or controls, to some degree, everything that happens both to humanity as a whole and to us as individuals. It is the basis for each and every one of arguments put forth by Iyov's so-called friends.

As I wrestled with the issues of providence, suffering, and evil, it has been helpful for me to differentiate between two kinds of evil. Human or moral evil is obviously the sort of suffering that we perpetrate on one another; natural evil is those natural phenomena that result in human suffering. Man-made suffering is intentional. Natural suffering is unintentional,

---

1. Faiths based on the Bible: Rabbinic Judaism, Christianity, Islam, Sikh, Baha'i, Latter Day Saints. The list goes on.

unless one believes in the traditional monotheistic Jewish-Christian-Islamic God-concept; then God, as creator and sustainer of all, is responsible for both kinds, although clearly less for the human evil because it is also believed that we humans exercise free will.

Many apologists for God's apparent inactivity and apathy in the face of human evil take refuge in the concept of free will, choosing to blame human beings completely for this kind of suffering—there are so many varieties, from domestic violence to sexual abuse to robbery, murder, mayhem, and genocide—and so let the Creator off the hook. But the rabbis of old, in their close reading of the Bible, nailed God's culpability even for human evil. In a midrash (rabbinic story) elaborating on Ca'in's murder of Hevel (Abel), God admits responsibility both for creating human beings with a flaw and for being an apathetic bystander. Responding to God's question "Where is your brother Hevel?," Ca'in retorts:

> You are he who is the guardian of all creatures and you ask of him from me? . . . I have killed him. But you created the evil inclination [*yetzer ha'ra*] in me. You are the guardian of everything, yet you allowed me to kill him. You are the one who killed him . . . for if you had accepted my sacrifice as you did his, I would not have grown jealous.[2]

God, in this midrash, acknowledges that Ca'in is right because the prooftext is read not just as a plea—"His blood cries out to me [*ely* אלי]"—but also as an accusation—"His blood cries out against me [*aly* עלי]"—because God had clearly violated one of his own commandments: "Do not stand upon the blood of your fellow."[3] According to this midrash, with regards to human evil, God is at least partially responsible, just as surely as the perpetrator of the wrong.

But if God is partially responsible for human evil, which is also the result of the exercise of our free will, then God as Creator must be even more responsible for natural evil, for which there are no mediating factors. As with human evil, natural evil comes in seemingly endless variety: from events on a grand scale—earthquakes, hurricanes, tsunamis and the like—to any number of debilitating diseases, even to death itself. Any death (perhaps excepting those that occur painlessly and quickly and those in

---

2. *Tanhuma*, Ber/Gen 9. See more on the evil inclination in Laytner, *Arguing with God*, 58–63, and the sources cited there.

3. Vay/Lev 19:16.

old age and relatively good health) and every illness are design flaws in the blueprint of Creation.

Mark Twain, that honest curmudgeon of a theologian, once wrote:

> Man starts in as a child and lives on diseases till the end, as a regular diet. He has mumps, measles, whooping cough, croup, tonsillitis, diphtheria, scarlet fever, almost as a matter of course. Afterward, as he goes along, his life continues to be threatened at every turn: by colds, coughs, asthma, bronchitis, itch, cholera, cancer, consumption, yellow fever, bilious fever, typhus fever, hay fever, ague, chilblains, piles, inflammation of the entrails, indigestion, toothache, earache, deafness, dumbness, blindness, influenza, chicken pox, cowpox, smallpox, liver complaint, constipation, bloody flux, warts, pimples, boils, carbuncles, abscesses, bunions, corns, tumors, fistulas, pneumonia, softening of the brain, melancholia and fifteen other kinds of insanity; dysentery, jaundice, diseases of the heart, the bones, the skin, the scalp, the spleen the kidneys, the nerves, the brain, the blood; scrofula, paralysis, leprosy, neuralgia, palsy, fits, headache, thirteen kinds of rheumatism, forty-six of gout, and a formidable supply of gross and unprintable disorders of one sort or another. Also—but why continue the list?[4]

4. Mark Twain, "Damned Human Race," in *Letters from the Earth*, 182. To update Mark Twain, here is this partial alphabetical list of just some of the kinds of cancer, from the National Cancer Center at the National Institutes of Health. Imagine if we tried to list all types and kinds of diseases!

> Acute Myeloid Leukemia, AIDS-Related Cancers, Bone Cancer, Brain Tumor, Breast Cancer, Cervical Cancer, Childhood Cancers, Colon Cancer, Colorectal Cancer, D [no Entries—thank God!], Endometrial Cancer, Esophageal Cancer, Eye Cancer, F [no entries—thank God!], Gallbladder Cancer, Gastric (Stomach) Cancer, Glioma, Head and Neck Cancer, Hodgkin's Lymphoma, Intraocular Melanoma, J [no entries—thank God!], Kaposi's Sarcoma, Kidney (Renal Cell) Cancer, Laryngeal Cancer, Lip and Oral Cavity Cancer, Liver Cancer, Lung Cancer, Lymphoma, Melanoma, Multiple Myeloma, Myelogenous Leukemia, Nasal Cavity and Paranasal Sinus Cancer, Non-Hodgkin's Lymphoma, Oral Cancer, Ovarian Cancer, Pancreatic Cancer, Parathyroid Cancer, Penile Cancer, Pituitary Tumor, Pregnancy and Breast Cancer, Pregnancy and Hodgkin's Lymphoma, Pregnancy and Non-Hodgkin's Lymphoma, Prostate Cancer, Q [no entries—praise God again!], Rectal Cancer, Renal Cell (Kidney) Cancer, Salivary Gland Cancer, Skin Cancer (non-Melanoma), Skin Cancer (Melanoma), Skin Carcinoma, Small Intestine Cancer, Stomach (Gastric) Cancer, Testicular Cancer, Thyroid Cancer, Urethral Cancer, Uterine Cancer, Vaginal Cancer, Vulvar Cancer, Waldenström's Macroglobulinemia, Wilms' Tumor, X, Y, Z [no entries—praise God yet again!].

The human condition itself is reason enough for people to be angry with God the Creator. All you have to do is visit a hospital to see there more problems inherent in the human body than you could ever imagine. True, there is healing there, and that is good, but without the design flaws of the human body, what need would there be for healing?

There is a midrash that states that since all of God's deeds are perfect, one ought not question why it is that we don't have three eyes or three legs or think of other ways that God's Creation might be improved upon.[5] I, however, think that we ought to imagine how things might have been—and three eyes would be only a beginning! (And don't even get me started on the planned obsolescence of the aging human body!) This is not the best of all possible worlds unless one lacks imagination.

Following Mark Twain's lead, one could make a huge list of all that is wrong with Creation and how it could stand improvement. Getting the Contractor to review the list of design flaws and to make repairs is quite another matter! But I'm willing to cut God some slack here: If God created as perfect a world as possible from the imperfect materials at hand, then he may be excused at least partially for some of Creation's problems. If, on the other hand, God created everything *ex nihilo* (out of nothing), then God has a major lawsuit on his hands for some serious design and structural flaws. Both with regards to moral evil and natural evil, God, as the Creator of all, is culpable.

This problem is further complicated by our inclination (or need) to see God's hand only in what we perceive as being good outcomes. For example, some years ago, a resident at a home for people living with AIDS, run by the agency I was directing, had a very positive response to his "drug cocktail" treatment. He was absolutely ecstatic about his new T-cell levels and went about the house shouting, "It's a miracle! Praise Jesus!" In truth, this fellow's renewed health was a miracle—but I had to speak privately to him to shush him because his "miracle" upset everyone else in the house who had not been similarly "blessed." Put another way, if God was responsible for this one individual's temporary improvement, was God similarly responsible for his housemates' continued poor health? Does your mind recoil from the possibility that God is the source of both?

Every time I watch survivors of some catastrophe being interviewed on television, or read about them in the newspaper, I cringe, waiting to hear "Thank God I was spared" or "The Lord was watching out for me."

---

5. *Ber/Gen Rabbah* 12:1.

But, although some survivors of a plane crash may attribute their survival to God's will—and many of us might have the same reaction were we in their shoes—most of us would probably shun the corollary that it must therefore also have been God's will that everyone else perish. The late Rev. Rod Romney, of Seattle First Baptist Church, told a story about how he and a carload of his fellow Baptist ministers narrowly averted a head-on collision, only because the oncoming car missed them and smashed into the car behind them. After a few minutes of shocked silence and blessed relief, one of his colleagues exclaimed, "God was certainly with us there!" Romney recalls that this remark was followed by a moment of silence, before someone realized the incongruity of that statement and replied, "Yeah, but he sure let the people in that other car have it." One shrinks from this conclusion, yet many people are willing to assert that, since the Creator operates with a plan, we must accept whatever happens as God's will, even perceived evils—although usually with the hoped-for caveat that they are not to happen to us. For the Rev. Romney, this was the beginning of his understanding "that often our talk about God's involvement in our lives is expressed in some rather stupid and incongruous images."[6] God, in the epilogue of the book of Iyov, is equally fed up: "I am incensed at you and your two friends, for you have not spoken the truth about me as did my servant Iyov."[7] This bears remembering as we look at some traditional rationalizations for the problem of suffering.

III A PLETHORA OF PLATITUDES

Suffering presents a conundrum to most people. In most religious traditions, including those of Asian origin, there *is* the belief that all that happens is part of a universal plan, whether that structure is karma or divine providence. According to these beliefs, everything is explainable precisely because it occurs as part of a universal order. Therefore, when bad things happen to good people, comfort and meaning ultimately may be obtained through acceptance of one's fate, knowing that God has ordained it for our own good or that it is the working out of our particular destinies. "Submission" is the term used in Islam, and it applies equally to other faiths as well.

However, if we truly believed this, why seek medical treatment, a human intervention, when God or karma has ordained that you be ill or

6. Romney, "Changing Faces of God."
7. Iyov 42:7.

healthy? Why even pray for healing if God has willed you otherwise? Obviously, most of us choose not to follow this line of thinking to its logical conclusion.

We may accept the principle that everything happens according to some providential plan, but we can't accept that bad things will happen to us for no apparent reason. Why? Because, down deep, we can't accept suffering without a good rationale (or rationalization). Consequently, particularly in the past, theologians and philosophers spent much effort to explain two sets of apparently contradictory beliefs, the first of which fits into the second: First, human beings have free will; but God is omniscient. Second, there is one God, who is omnipotent and perfectly good; but evil happens. Theologians call the attempt to vindicate or reconcile divine providence with the existence of evil "theodicy." Of course, if you take away the idea that God is in charge, then the problem disappears and what happens is just good or bad fortune.

Put another way, we probably all can agree that "shit happens" in life. It is an experiential given, a reality. We know shit when we smell it—and we know it when we are living through it. Many rationalizations (theodicies) have been written in a futile effort to sanitize this problem but, unfortunately, to assert that "bad things" are actually "good things" is like pretending that shit isn't shit. One *can* tell the difference. To pretend otherwise would be like taking leave of one's senses! Nonetheless, the efforts persist.

Over the centuries, each faith has developed a number of solutions to this dilemma, so that today (switching to a more appetizing metaphor) a sufferer has a veritable smorgasbord of rationalizations from which to choose. When I went to sample this feast, I measured each offering by how it tasted, specifically whether or not it masked the bitter taste in my mouth left by the Holocaust. For me, as a Jew, the Holocaust remains the zenith of human cruelty to other humans and the nadir of divine activity in the face of immense human suffering. The Holocaust poses a challenge to the validity of any of these theodicies because it applies our concepts of God and prayer, and suffering and providence, to the most extreme of life situations. This is what I call the "Holocaust litmus test": *Whatever your key theological concepts are, they must not only apply to your own life; the challenge is that they also make sense of Auschwitz.*[8]

8. This is my version of my teacher (and first employer) Yitz Greenberg's "working principle," a kind of moral plumb line by which post-Holocaust theological claims should be measured: that no statement, theological or otherwise, should be made about the Holocaust that would not be credible in the presence of burning children.

Here is a taste of some major explanations for suffering, primarily from the Abrahamic faith traditions, along with the reasons why I object to them—and may the scholars of religion forgive me for generalizing:

1. The most ancient but still current of biblical answers views suffering as punishment for sins committed. Suffering is seen as a loving discipline—like corporal punishment—meant to redirect the sinner to follow God's ways. It is also expiatory, meaning that the actual suffering makes amends for the sins committed—as in "Jesus died for our sins" or the sacrificial cult in ancient Israel. According to this view, one must accept such suffering as divinely ordained punishment and then analyze one's behavior for sin and make the necessary changes. In the Bible, this view was applied both collectively and individually.[9] This explanation is still found in the traditional Jewish prayer book and echoed in popular Jewish-Christian-Islamic theology down through the ages.

I reject this explanation of suffering. It blames the victim. After World War II and the Holocaust, with sixty million killed and millions more scarred for life—I'm talking both Jews and non-Jews here—this response to suffering is simply obscene. First, because it casts doubt on the character of the Judge and can lead to accusations that God is an abusive deity.[10] Second, because no sin is great enough to warrant the alleged punishment. And third, because it presumes to know the mind of God in this matter. This last objection warrants more attention.

Too often, this rationalization is invoked by religious leaders who claim to know God's will. Usually their understanding of events reinforces their own belief system. One time I heard a sermon by an Orthodox rabbi about some Israeli soldiers. They were on tank patrol and the time came for morning prayers. Only one soldier was traditionally observant and he insisted that they stop so that he could go outside, don his *tefillin* (phylacteries), and say his prayers. While he was praying, the others remained in

9. On punishments and rewards for adhering to the Covenant, see for example Mish/Prov 3:33; 10:3; 11:8, 19; 12:21; 13:21; the blessings and curses in Vay/Lev 26 and Dvar/Deut 28; the running commentary in the books of Yeho/Josh, Shof/Judg, and Mel/Kgs; and the warnings in most of the prophetic books. For suffering as discipline, see Mish/Prov 3:11–12. Note that in their early formulation, rewards and punishments are collective but by the time of the First Exile prophets and other writings were postulating only individual responsibility—see, for example, Yehez/Ezek 18:1–4; Yerm/Jer 31:29–30; and Eicha/Lam 5:7. For a summary of this perspective and other biblical theodicies, see Ehrman, *God's Problem*. For a detailed analysis of traditional Jewish perspectives on suffering, see Kraemer, *Responses to Suffering* and Birnbaum, *God and Evil*, 3–50.

10. For more on God as an abuser, see Blumenthal, *Facing the Abusing God*.

the tank, smoking and talking. Suddenly, seemingly out of nowhere, a shell hit the tank, incinerating all those inside. The rabbi's message: Only the religiously observant Jew was spared from death because he was observing one of God's commandments. The others perished because they weren't.

People like this are likely also to invoke God's "creation" or "use" of HIV as a means of condemning those afflicted with the disease—in their minds, people who are sinners already: gay men, IV drug users, promiscuous people, prostitutes. Would they go so far as to deny these "sinners" medical or pastoral care since it would go against God's presumed will? I sometimes wonder.

This sort of thinking transcends religions and ideologies. After the 9/11 attacks on the New York World Trade Center and the Pentagon, Osama bin Laden proclaimed that the terrorists had succeeded because America was evil and God was aligned with those who sought to fight this evil empire. Similarly, albeit from a very different religious orientation, the late Rev. Jerry Falwell, with the Rev. Pat Robertson voicing agreement, blamed civil liberties groups, feminists, gays and lesbians, abortionists and pagans for provoking God's anger, thereby causing God to "lift the curtain and allow the enemies of America to give us probably what we all deserve," namely, the terrorist attacks on the World Trade Center and the Pentagon. However, by making God ultimately responsible for this tragedy, the reverends joined in theological company with bin Laden and other Muslim extremists, who also believed that America had incurred divine anger and deserved what it got. By remaining theologically consistent, these clergymen made God responsible for the deaths of over three thousand innocent souls.

There also were people who tried to rationalize the terrifying randomness of the 2004 Southeast Asian tsunami by injecting the deity into the event. Some stated that it happened because the victims hadn't accepted Jesus; others pronounced that it happened because the dead weren't good enough Muslims; still others pontificated that it was bad karma or choice of wrong livelihood. But I don't believe that God was in the big wave. What happened was a purely mechanistic occurrence of nature. For those who died, it was their tragic misfortune to be in the wrong place at the wrong time, and for those who survived, they were damned lucky—and with regards to the rest of humanity, it was an opportunity to be able to help the survivors recover, if we so chose.

Looking for God's hand in history or current events or even natural disasters is a time-honored tradition. Curiously, for most of those who

believe in a God who uses natural phenomena or human activity as punitive instruments, such divinely ordained evils never seem to afflict them
directly but almost miraculously only someone else. It's always easier to
judge from afar.

There are grave dangers involved in this kind of causal thinking even
if it does provide theological certainty. It is a theodicy with extremely troubling consequences. It is also both wrong and unjust if God, in Avraham's
words, "brings death upon the innocent as well as the guilty, so that the
innocent and the guilty fare alike."[11] It is distressing to believe that God
would utilize some of his putative servants to slaughter other human beings. It is inconceivable that God would save some worthy souls from a
disaster while allowing other equally worthy souls to perish or that God
would strike some people with terminal diseases for no apparent reason
and not others. It is equally monstrous that God would afflict some of the
relatively righteous yet pass over (or seemingly even reward) those who are
truly wicked. So this theodicy is in fact very harmful to God's image and
reputation. It is also harmful to people. *One can do serious harm to other
human* beings *in presuming to know the mind of God and then telling them
why they suffer.* Once someone claims to know God's will, it can lead to
all kinds of violence, from the shunning of people living with AIDS to the
bombing of abortion clinics to religious terrorism.

2. Suffering can also be seen as a test or trial of individual faith, such as
Avraham or Iyov was subjected to. If one can endure it without losing faith
and maintain one's trust in God, one will emerge spiritually more refined
(not to mention being rewarded appropriately). Imagery from the Jewish
tradition includes comparing the tested soul to smelted metal, which becomes purer through fire; a tree, which grows healthier through pruning; a
clay pot that gets knocked to test its mettle; or a fire that, once poked, burns
with renewed energy.

Since God only tests those presumably worthy, it should be considered an honor to be chosen for "testing"—and God "never gives one more
than one can handle." Furthermore, since God only tests the righteous, one
ought to accept these afflictions with loving acceptance. In the Jewish tradition, this sort of suffering is called "sufferings of love."

A corollary to this perspective affirms that the righteous suffer in this
world in order to inherit the World to Come. If you believe in an afterlife,
then indeed this reward can counterbalance suffering. However, after the

11. Ber/Gen 18:23–25.

Holocaust, this theodicy also is simply obscene because both the test and the character of the Examiner pale in comparison to the numbers of dead and the suffering both they and the survivors endured. And as to the reward at the End of Time—who knows?

3. Some people assert the inexplicability of suffering in combination with an attitude of submission. Individuals are encouraged to place their trust in God's goodness and in God's plan for each of us, even if it includes suffering. Whatever happens, whether good or bad, is God's will and God alone knows the reason. Therefore, a person simply ought to submit to God's inscrutable will and realize that whatever happens is for the best because it is divinely ordained. Having an attitude of "Don't ask" is appropriate because questioning demonstrates a lack of trust or faith in God's plan. (It's also appropriate since "don't ask" inevitably invites a "won't tell" on God's part.)

In a way I admire those who truly believe that God is in the details; that God is intimately involved in the life experiences of each and every human being. It makes for a safer world, a more childlike world, with a protective Parent hovering nearby. I admire their trust and envy their faith, but shake my head at their apparent naïveté and denial of obvious experience. Nonetheless, many people find comfort in this explanation and I must say that there *is* something very comforting about surrendering control of your life to God. It is capable of sustaining inner peace even in the face of great suffering. It keeps your world safe, secure, and predictable even when life's experiences may well suggest otherwise. And perhaps there *is* a divine plan in which both personal and national suffering makes sense. Perhaps the good suffer in this world for sins committed and *are* rewarded in the Hereafter, whereas the wicked may prosper now but will pay later. Perhaps there *is* "a divine integrity beyond our knowing" but, after the Holocaust, this response to suffering also is very offensive because what kind of God and divine plan can involve the deaths of six million Jews, not to mention tens of millions of other people? And that was just one genocide and one war. For that matter, what kind of God and divine plan can allow for the untimely death of even one individual?

Hindus and Buddhists also promote acceptance of suffering but offer a different providential plan. In the Hindu-Buddhist traditions, life's experiences—suffering and pleasure, joy and sadness—are ultimately illusory, but life itself entails suffering. Part of life's illlusory nature is the result of our living through a series of reincarnations, and what happens in one life is partially the result of actions in previous lives. This is the process of *karmaphala*. A person's spiritual task is to attempt to comprehend the reality that exists behind the illusion by aiming for enlightenment—the transcendence (or extinction) of all passions and attachments—and liberation, which ends the cycle of rebirths. How a person responds to suffering—how s/he experiences it—can affect one's long-term *karma* and therefore can help on one's way to liberation from the bonds of this illusory world. Following the various Hindu ways toward enlightenment or the Buddha's Noble Eightfold Path can speed this liberation process.

When something bad happens to someone in these faith traditions—for example, the death of a child—it would be understood as acculmated bad *karma* from a previous life, and one should accept the "judgment" of this *karma*. But if a child dies, whose *karma* is affected? The child is most directly affected, so s/he must really have been bad in a previous life; but the parents suffer too, although not with their lives, so each must have been somewhat bad. Or perhaps *karma* works its way on both simultaneously? It would be hard to know.

But *karma* as reward or punishment gives a rather profound reality to suffering that contradicts its purported illusoriness. As popularly practiced, the suffering that *karma* produces can be doubly real. Not only does the individual actually suffer, but s/he may also suffer socially as well because when bad things do happen in this life, it follows that one *must* have done wrong in a previous life—so sometimes suffering people are rejected or shunned by others for being past-life sinners. It's a problem.

4. One traditional Christian option holds that although God is omnipotent, God/Jesus chooses not to use that power in a broken unredeemed world but instead is present with us in the ordeals we suffer, even to the point of suffering with us. When we suffer, we share something with Jesus, because in human form he suffered as we do. Suffering makes human beings the wounded hands and feet of Jesus. Some believe that the more one suffers, the more one is adding to Christ's glory. It is certainly comforting, in a way, to know one is not alone in one's suffering and that one shares this with God, but one has to ask: "So what? What is the tangible benefit of God suffering along with us? Where is justice? And why did God need Jesus to suffer in the first place? Why did God intervene previously in the past but not for Jesus and not for us now?"

5. Then there are a number of theories that limit the power of God. All of these have attractive features but all are problematic too.

Some Christian denominations embrace the existence of "Satan" as an opposing power to God. Good things come from God; bad things come from the devil, a semi-deity. This perspective is shared by dualistic religions such as Zoroastrianism and various polytheistic religions. According to this view, human life becomes the battleground between two or more cosmic forces and one prays to the good God(s) for support and strength against the bad. As a monotheist, I reject this duality of power—although it is very tempting to see the Nazis and their allies as demonic rather than human, and their power as deriving from some dark source.

According to Jewish mysticism, Creation couldn't contain the emanations of divine light that God used in the beginning and its vessels shattered, resulting in an imperfect world with a variety of evils. Our job is to act as God's partners by gathering the shards of divine light through our deeds, ultimately assisting God in restoring perfection to the world (*tikkun olam*). I love this mythic story but I have to ask: Was Creation a mistake or a merely a miscalculation on God's part? Six days apparently can make for sloppy work!

A deist solution asserts that God is like a watchmaker who, after making the world, withdrew from the field of action to let the "machine" run on its own. God's general providence is operational in nature but it doesn't extend to the personal level. Albert Einstein once said that God does not play dice with the universe. To say this is to affirm that a basic sense of order can be observed but I would amend Einstein's aphorism, adding "but the game can be very hard on the bit players." There may be an order apparent in nature, even in how earthquakes and hurricanes operate, but the random chaos that results from catastrophic natural phenomena can be awfully hard on people and other living creatures. Thus, to some kind of general global providence I say, "Maybe; probably even yes," but to personal providence I say, "Show me the evidence. How does it work?" It really isn't too much to ask . . . besides, I'd like to know what God has been doing since finishing the work of Creation and setting things in motion.

Some philosophers suggest that God cannot be omnipotent for then we would have *no* power. Rather, God is relatively omnipotent, meaning he has limited powers and so is neither responsible for what happens nor capable of intervening. It is totally in our hands, with God only "urging" us on to do good.[12] Can this God save us from harm? Is this a God to worship?

---

12. Jonas, "Concept of God after Auschwitz." For an example of a process theology theodicy, see Griffin, *God, Power, and Evil.*

(Which is not to dismiss this perspective, only to point out its contradiction of traditional expectations of God.)

Lastly, a "New Age" or "New Thought" perspective would suggest that we are what we think. If we want wealth or health, focus on these; but if we think sick, we get sick and if we think suffering, we suffer. There is a certain truth to this because we do shape—and thus to a certain degree do control—our inner realities, but the power of positive thinking does have its limits. Death camp inmates might have been able to free their minds but they couldn't think themselves free of their physical situations.

Theologians and philosophers keep on coming up with new rationalizations to torment the sufferer and tickle God's funny bone.[13] Of these, one critic noted that their books are "far removed from the actual pain and suffering that takes place in our world, dealing with evil as an 'idea' rather than an experienced reality that rips apart people's lives."[14] All too often it seems to me that theologians are more concerned about reconciling their theodicies with their preconceived theologies or dogmatic convictions than in looking for a soul-satisfying way of dealing with the problem of evil.

As long as we cling to the traditional ways of looking at the issue of God and suffering, our world will remain awash with bad rationalizations. Scottish theologian John Swinton, of the University of Aberdeen, has called for a paradigm shift in how we deal with the problems of evil and suffering, away from trying to explain them to presenting ways they can be resisted and transformed. He calls this "pastoral" or "practical" theodicy, a theodicy of action that focuses on practices people can learn and embody in order to resist evil, transform suffering, and be faithful to the ideals of their faith.[15] I value his perspective and endorse his idea because of its pragmatic focus on the human being.

The Holocaust, for me, has created an irreversible rift between the religious past, with its rationalizations for suffering, and the present, with its questions. I do not believe that those who perished at the hands of the Nazis deserved the suffering they experienced. I do not believe their individual or collective suffering was some kind of divine testing of their mettle or a purging of sin. I do not believe that God chose to save this one or that

13. For some summaries of contemporary theodicies, see Griffin, *God, Power, and Evil* and Barry Whitney, *What Are They Saying about God and Evil?*

14. Ehrman, *God's Problem*, 18.

15. Swinton, *Raging with Compassion*. Harold Kushner makes a similar point from a Jewish perspective in *Why Bad Things Happen to Good People*, 132–48.

one, while choosing or permitting others to die. I do not believe that a good God would allow the deaths of millions of people as part of some inscrutable divine plan. And I don't want to speculate about the nature of God or the origins of Creation. I would rather suffer the agony of unknowing than choose to rely on any of these gnarled answers. I want to see an end to the rationalizations, an end to theodicy.

IV TOWARD A DIFFERENT UNDERSTANDING OF SUFFERING

In order to try making sense of the suffering I had observed in history and experienced in life, I found it helpful to affirm four key principles or ideas. The first is to re-embrace radical monotheism, in which everything has its source in God; the second is to affirm that there is no apparent causality between the evils that befall us and God; third, that we must provide our own meaning to our suffering; and fourth, that we ought to cultivate a sense of inner balance at all times.

Radical Monotheism

In the Tanakh (the Jewish Bible, similar to the Christian Old Testament), God is the source of everything, even those things that, in our estimation, are called evil. To cite but one example of many,[16] the prophet called Yeshayahu (Isaiah) has God declare: "I am YHVH and there is none else. I form light and create darkness, I make peace [well-being] and *create evil*. I, YHVH, do all these things."[17] This is the core of radical monotheism; radical because it stands in contradiction to the popular belief that only good things come from God. In radical monotheism, God is the source of all.

---

16. Eicha/Lam 3:38 and Iyov/Job 2:10 assert that God is the source of both good and evil. In 1 Shm/Sam 16:14–23 God sends an evil spirit to torment *Sha'ul*/Saul, and *Ahm/* Amos 3:6 affirms rhetorically that God is the one who sends evil on a city.

17. Yesh/Isa 45:6–7. Centuries later, the rabbis incorporated this line into the daily liturgy, but with a significant change. Although they still considered God the author of all, they felt it necessary to downplay—if only for liturgical purposes—the fact that perceived evil also could come from God, so they changed the line to read: "Praised are you, Lord [YHVH] our God, ruler of the universe, who forms light and creates darkness, who makes peace and *creates all [things].*"

Iyov declaimed at the beginning of his ordeal ,"Should we accept only the good from God and not accept evil?"[18] Following his lead, the ancient rabbis sought to promote an attitude towards suffering that unequivocally held God responsible for all things, ordering that "A person is obligated to utter a blessing for the bad just as one utters a blessing for the good."[19] As a radical monotheist, I accept this premise and embrace the conundrum that God is the author of all. But what does it really mean to affirm that God is responsible for both the good and the bad? What are the implications in our lives?

People who can suspend their critical thinking and accept that everything happens according to some beneficent divine plan may have an easier time accepting that everything comes from God, but most people, including me, only want to see God in the good and the beautiful. Although the rabbis decreed that we should thank God for the bad that happens to us as well as the good, I find this almost impossible to do when bad things happen. How contrary this is to human nature—or at least to *this* human's nature! I have no problem thanking God for all the good in my life; but the troubles and woes too? That is still too far of a spiritual stretch for me— even if I accept that God is the source of all.

It is always easy to see the wonder of Creation in a sunset or in a forest grove, in a newborn baby or when making love; it is almost trite to thank God when smelling a beautiful flower or seeing a spectacular vista. But it is quite another matter to appreciate the beauty in things when surrounded by a swarm of mosquitoes or to thank God for germs and bacteria that are the cause of suffering to many. Once, while working with people with AIDS, I was driving in my car and listening to an NPR *Fresh Air* radio interview by Terri Gross with Dr. David Baltimore, then head of the National Institutes of Health's AIDS Vaccine Advisory Council. Although this was back in 1999, I remember it to this day because what he said struck me deeply. Dr. Baltimore talked about the HIV virus in terms that can only be described as reverential: how amazing it was in structure and how ingeniously it worked. Here was a person dedicated to eradicating this horrible virus yet, in a weird way, at the same time he was in awe of this minute

18. Iyov 2:10.

19. Or as one rabbi has God say in a midrash: "Do not behave towards me as the heathens behave towards their gods . . . [Rather] If I bring happiness upon you give thanks, and when I bring sufferings give thanks also." See also *b. Berachot* 19a, 33b, 54a, 60b; *Megillah* 25a; *Pesachim* 50a; and the *Tziduk HaDin* prayer of the Jewish funeral service, and my *Arguing with God*, 103–15.

particle of Creation; he could marvel at its intricate natural design even as he sought to destroy it. That is radical monotheism.

When I look at the world, I see that Creation has its apparent flaws as well as its observable beauties but, overall, I think that Creation itself, though morally neutral, is generally speaking and overall "good."[20] From our limited and self-interested perspective, we say that some events are good and others not but—as God pointed out to Iyov—we know diddly-squat about how the system operates as a whole.[21] It is important to remember that none of us is the center of the universe, even if our self-centered, narcissistic being tries to claim otherwise.

Whether an event is good or bad is a matter of perceptions—it is based on how we process or interpret life experiences at any given moment. The same sun whose light I consider a blessing here in Seattle may simultaneously be someone else's cursed drought-maker. Whose view is correct? Neither person's. It is only a matter of perspective—and even that view may change as we change. What we really mean when we say a certain experience is bad is that it appears to be bad for us *at a particular point in time*.

Thus, the ultimate challenge for spiritual people is to be able to appreciate the mystery and wonder—the awe-fullness—of an earthquake or a disease, even as one is struck by horror and sadness. It is hard to reconcile these two aspects of natural evil—the wonder with the terror—yet it is essential to do so in order to acknowledge unity of all things under God's oneness. In the Tanakh, the Hebrew word i-r-a ירא means both "fear" and "awe" and it is often used with reference to God. Traditionally, God combines both. This too is radical monotheism.

---

20. See Ber/Gen 1.

21. My wife, Richelle Harrell, who has had her share of premonitions, flashes of *déjà vu*, and serendipitous experiences (which she calls miraculous), challenges me to consider that these sorts of experiences show that the world is more complex and layered than it seems. I can't explain these paranormal phenomena but I also don't discount or dismiss them either. I can live with their remaining tantalizingly inexplicable. They remind me that the book of Iyov operates on two levels: the level of the wager made between God and *HaSattan*, and the level of Iyov and his friends. The latter lived and talked in ignorance of the greater reality and Iyov only became aware of it after God put in an appearance.

No Causality

Equally important to me is the rejection of a belief that is almost bred in the bone: I force myself *to choose not to make* any causal connection between what happens in life and God, who is the source of all. What this means in practical terms is that I believe there is a high degree of randomness to life in terms of who is killed in an earthquake or who survives a car crash, or who gets AIDS or cancer and who survives. Even when it comes to human evils, in the end they often affect innocent lives just as randomly as natural evils do. They all have their source in God yet none is caused by God.

Of course, events that might be perceived as miracles do happen. One person might inexplicably be cured of cancer; another might survive a massacre. Both likely would call their salvation miraculous and they would be right to do so in the sense that it is inexplicable and incredibly lucky. But I draw the line when it comes to asserting that God was responsible. I strive to marvel at the totality of Creation, even at the terrible awesome power of so-called natural evils and the awfulness of human evils, but I never ascribe their occurrence to God's will. What happens seems mostly a matter of chance—dumb luck—and the choices we make as a result. Put more simply: Life is a crapshoot; what matters only is that you try to go with the roll and mitigate any negative consequences.

Making Meaning

Because life appears to be a process of random chaos, with no rhyme or reason to it, I am challenged to provide my own meaning to its events. I believe a life experience acquires meaning solely by what we choose to impose on the experience and on what we learn from that experience, for better or for worse.

In *Man's Search for Meaning*, Victor Frankl observed that Jews incarcerated in Nazi concentration camps stood a better chance of surviving (assuming they weren't carted off to the gas chambers) if they were able to imbue their lives with meaning.[22] The same holds true for people with chronic and terminal medical conditions and people dealing with grief issues.

---

22. My friend Bruce Kochis pointed out that what kept Frankl going in the camp was his book and the love of his wife.

Many a person with AIDS told me that only getting that terrible diagnosis made them turn their lives around and cease their self-destructive behaviors. Their impending deaths often gave their lives meaning and purpose—usually to educate others about preventing the spread of the disease or encouraging people to volunteer their time and energy. This search for meaning is a way to transcend the tragedy of our most terrible personal experiences. In meaning lies purpose, and in purpose there is hope, and hope feeds life.

Why do some people suffer more than others? I am not referring here about physical pain, although that too is experienced differently by each of us, but rather about emotional struggle and spiritual suffering. When something "bad" happens, it presents a challenge to one's personal integrity, i.e., one's sense of wholeness, and to the meaning one finds in, or provides to, that experience.

There have been numerous Jewish, Christian, and Muslim martyrs who died gruesome deaths yet never suffered spiritually. They did not because they knew they were more than their bodies, that their lives and deaths were part of something larger, and they had faith or trust that there was an order to their world—a belief in a divine plan and in a World to Come that could sustain them even when in unimaginable physical pain. Their sense of connectedness with God never wavered and that gave them hope; it allowed them to maintain their wholeness.

Now consider the case of Iyov. Iyov was a righteous man who suffered spiritually because he could not reconcile his experience with the commonplace perception that suffering only came as a result of sin. After being afflicted with tragedy and physical suffering, he also endured spiritual suffering, induced in large measure after his so-called friends began to "comfort" him. This led him to question God's justice as it applied to his personal situation. Iyov suffered because his sense of meaning in life was turned upside down. He could not accept what had happened because it made no sense based on his understanding of how the world was supposed to operate, and he did not have the inner strength to cope with adversity *and* the torment of his friends' insensitivity. As a result, he suffered spiritual alienation—a sense of isolation from God's presence.

Fortunately for Iyov—and how unlike so many of us!—he received an answer directly from God. From his revelatory experience, Iyov learned that a) what had happened to him was an insignificant part of the greater mystery of Creation, b) that it had nothing to do with justice, and c) that

God cared enough to put in a personal appearance. It was the divine appearance that restored Job's sense of connectedness with God even though the lesson learned—that there is no justice manifest in suffering and that what occurs in life is part of something so vast that one can never comprehend it—was at best cold comfort. Creation is too vast, too complex, for us to comprehend in its totality. A little humility was called for in Iyov's case, just as it is in ours. But at the same time, as God later notes, it was Iyov who in his anger had spoken appropriately of God, not his friends, who spouted the popular theodicies/rationalizations of their era.

Like Iyov, the ancient rabbis believed in asking big questions. Why, they wondered, did the Torah begin with the letter *beit* ב, the second letter of the Hebrew alphabet, reasoning that the first word of the Bible should more fittingly begin with the first letter of the alphabet, the *aleph* א. One answer proposed was the following: That just as the letter *beit* is enclosed on three sides but open on the fourth, so too is our ability to know. Consequently, the Torah begins not with mysteries that remain closed to us, like: "Who is God?" "Why did God create?" "From what did God create?" "How did God create?" Rather, it opens with the creation of the cosmos itself, then moves to the creation of life on this planet, then to human life, and ultimately to history and us. The letter *beit* teaches that we cannot ever truly know what is above us, or what below us, or even what is behind us—we can only know that the way open to us lies ahead.

Life is like the letter *beit*. We get no answers looking above or below or even behind. The only option for us is what we make of it now, how we live it. Whatever happens to us in life is what it is; whatever we make of it is what it will mean. The meaning of suffering is not found by asking "Why?" but by asking "To what end?" or "What's the invitation in this experience?" A pregnant woman endures the pain of childbirth because she knows (or hopes) that something good will emerge, that a baby will be born. But other sorts of pain—physical and emotional and spiritual—are not so clearly productive. It remains for us to shape the offspring of that experience.

Do you "find" meaning in an experience of suffering or do you "make" meaning for such an experience? The difference is profound. The former implies that the meaning exists in the experience, perhaps even that God has something specific in mind in whatever happens to each and every one of us. The latter, on the other hand, suggests that experience itself is a *tabula rasa*, a blank slate, on which we can inscribe, or create, whatever meaning we wish, for good or bad, for life or death.

Suffering is a fearsome teacher. Some people lose faith in the course of suffering; others gain it. Some people are destroyed by the experience; others manage to heal. People who suffer physically may or may not suffer spiritually. I have seen both. Working with people with AIDS, I saw some transform their pain into creative, positive energy; but I also saw others turn their suffering in on themselves and wither from within. Our personal contexts may not be so extreme, but we all make this same choice, for better or for worse, at many different points in our lives, because living is a series of choices, of certain potentialities or possibilities pursued and others denied. Every experience is either a stepping-stone or a millstone, depending on how we respond to it, how we reflect on it, and how we use it.

Cultivating Inner Balance

According to the concept of the stages of grief, either Kübler-Ross's or some other model, "acceptance" is one of the final steps in the emotional healing process. Like the cycle of grief, suffering has its stages in which anger is as appropriate as acceptance. The goal ultimately is "acceptance," which means making spiritual peace with one's changed situation. Most people go through a series of emotional/spiritual peaks and valleys that mark their back-and-forth struggle to deal with grief or adversity.

However, in many of our faith traditions fatalism is often confused with faith and acquiescence with acceptance. For many people, displaying a lack of emotion during times of emotional or spiritual turmoil—and thereby denying anger, depression, and the like—may actually demonstrate fatalism, not faith; not acceptance of what has happened but acquiescence to an apparent abusive power beyond their control; not serenity but the suppression of honest grief and anger. The result is that many people consider passivity and the repression of "negative" feelings to be the proper responses to suffering of a truly pious person. We may aspire to respond like martyrs when "bad" things happen to us and then berate ourselves (or others) for reacting like Iyov, outraged at God for what has befallen us.

I would never suggest that it is goodly, or godly, to suffer in silence or that we should squelch our emotions in times of trouble. We human beings have every right to be upset if our expectations in life get thwarted by the random attacks of disease or death. In most cycles of grief, there is also a place for anger and protest; why not for people of faith too? For Jews, this concept might not be as foreign as it may be to other peoples because we have good role models of protest down through the ages. I believe in the value of argument and protest because they can help reorient ourselves in a period of crisis and turmoil. To lament or protest against one's fate or that of a loved one is the opposite of resignation; it is an assertion of self and power exactly at a time when the events are conspiring to rob you of both. Protest and anger can be good tools—if they help us transition to the stage of accepting that what is, is.

Suffering can be a lonely state of being. It can alienate you from your body; it can alienate you from other people; it can alienate you from your sense of connection with God. Isolation in all these ways only makes suffering worse. The challenge for those of us who accompany loved ones on these dolorous journeys is to keep our lips shut and our hearts open, so that the person at the center of the storm can voice the concerns of his or her soul, regardless of how they sound to our ears.

The key to providing suffering with positive meaning *is* acceptance. When life is taken as it is—when you release yourself from your expectations for the future and from your illusion of control—then you can begin the birthing process of transforming what was into what is, and let what will be, be. But it is not easy to do.

Personally, I try to cultivate internal balance regardless of what happens in my life. Equanimity would be an appropriate word as long as one understands this to be an inner state of being rather than maintaining outward composure, because anger, tears, laughter, and every other emotion have been my steps along the way towards an acceptance of what has happened and a return to the world of the living.[23]

A Christian minister friend—I wish I could remember who it was— once told me that, in her tradition, she was taught "to look for the grace in everything," meaning that God gives us something to learn from every experience, even bad ones. It seems to me that there is a certain psychological value and spiritual wisdom in "looking for the grace in everything" or "praising God for the good and the bad" because by doing this kind of reflection one may come to an eventual acceptance of whatever has happened.

---

23. My dear friend Deborah Bogin Cohen shared these words, attributed to Sir William Osler, about equanimity that describe my sense of the word exactly: "the Latin word *aequanimatas*... means 'calmness of mind' or 'inner peace.' Inner peace is certainly the ultimate resource for those dealing with suffering on a daily basis. But this isn't something achieved by distancing yourself from the suffering around you. Inner peace is more a question of cultivating perspective, meaning, and wisdom even as life touches you with its pain. It is more a spiritual quality than a mental quality."

I believe that nothing that happens comes directly from God, yet I see no contradiction between my Christian friend's affirmation and my own. To my mind, these apparently contradictory ideas are two sides of the same coin. To believe that nothing comes directly from God is almost the same as believing that everything comes from God. Both attitudes can lead to a state of acceptance. In my own time of crisis, I found I could almost repeat the words of Iyov: "YHVH [the LORD] has given, and YHVH has taken away; blessed be the name YHVH," except that I uttered: "The process of life gives and the process of life takes away; blessed be the process of life."

Whether one understands what happens in life to be part of God's plan or not, that is for each of us to decide for ourselves. But, regardless of how you achieve it, acquiring a sense of acceptance of your fortune can make suffering endurable, and perceiving a sense of unity with a divine presence can suffuse suffering with hope for a better future.

The founder of Multifaith Works, my mentor, the late Rev. Gwen Beighle, once told me how she dealt with spiritual pain—not only that of the many people she visited who were living with and dying from AIDS but also her own issues resulting from terminal ovarian cancer. She taught: "The Twenty-Third Psalm says: 'Yea though I walk through the valley of the shadow of death I will fear no evil, for you are with me.' It does not say that we will not suffer. But it does say that, as we go through suffering, God is somehow present with us to comfort us. Knowing this can help us accept what is happening." This interpretation of suffering worked for Gwen, who modeled how one can overcome a tragic situation (ovarian cancer) to die with grace and dignity, faith and hope. Hers was the most peaceful dying I ever was privileged to witness. I can only hope to die as good a death.

As for me, I find my comfort—and my meaning—in a God who may hopefully "accompany" me in some mysterious way throughout my life's experiences but who apparently directs nothing; a God who may "listen" when I pray but who apparently does nothing in response. In my God's non-action I may find strength and solace, but I find my comfort—and my meaning—in relying on myself and on my fellow human beings to do on earth that which many have expected God to do for them. If God's presence is anywhere, it is found in the midst of our individual and collective responses to life's challenges. With this evolving sense of God and this understanding of suffering, I am personally better able to deal with the random terrors of life.

The Hebrew word for "whole" (*shalem*) and the word for "peace" (*shalom*) share the same root (*sh-l-m* שלם), as does the Hebrew expression *refuah shleimah*, meaning "get better" but literally "a whole (or complete) healing." Like the modern understanding of the cycle of grief, the Jewish model for recovery is a circle, with a return to wholeness and peace being the desired ends.[24] In the end, my healing came through striving for equanimity amidst the buffeting of life, by seeking the spiritual learning moment in every experience, and in remaining connected with the divine.

24. My colleague, dear friend, and editor *par excellence* Mary Jane Francis points out that the Greek word *soso*, which means "to save," also means "to heal" and that in Christianity the term "salvation" includes health, healing, and wholeness.

Chapter 4

To Pray as Iyov Prayed
My Problem with Normative Prayer

"I cry out to you, but you do not answer me; / I wait, but you do not consider me. / You have become cruel to me; / With your powerful hand you harass me." (Iyov 30:20, 21)

I   MY PROBLEM WITH PRAYER

THE ISSUE OF HOW to understand suffering is closely tied to the role of prayer, especially petitionary prayer, which asks God to intercede to do what is requested. While our family was in the midst of its dark night, some of us turned to uttering prayers for divine intervention. But none of these pleas for healing were answered—at least not in the way that we wanted. This, for me, ended whatever residual attachment I had for this type of prayer. I finally came to accept that petitionary prayer doesn't pass my own "Holocaust litmus test" because our mundane requests for divine intervention made no sense in the light of how weightier prayers—the life-in-the-face-of-death appeals uttered by people in situations like Auschwitz—were ignored.

Blame my problem on the Bible. Simply stated, the stories of God's miraculous interventions into history as recorded in the Bible stand in stark contradiction to the darker realities of human life ever since. The two contradict each other. *Either* God's intervention during the Exodus from Egypt is somehow true *or* subsequent historical experience is true, but both can't be true without something having to give way. The contradiction shows the classic dilemma of theodicy. At issue is God's consistency.

If both are right, that would mean that on one occasion God chose to intervene while at another time God chose not to, or that at one time God acted with compassion but at another time God chose not to. To hold that both are true leaves God open to charges of being cruel and heartless, indifferent to human suffering, and deaf to pleas for mercy. And let me say it: A capricious God, or a cruel and abusive God, is worse than none at all!

The Exodus story has always been in tension with the suffering of the present. That tension exists because people refuse to let go of the hope for divine succor based on the past precedent of the Exodus yet there is also no escaping from the reality of their experience of suffering. Thinking with a global perspective, one could say that a "covenant of blood" exists among all the victims and survivors of mass murder and genocide, among those who prayed and waited in vain for divine intervention to save them.

This, in a nutshell is my problem with prayer as it pertains to suffering: To put it crassly, can we really expect that God—who apparently ignored the prayers of the many people who died in the Holocaust, or in Cambodia, Bosnia, Rwanda, Darfur, or anywhere else (sadly the list goes on and on)—will pay attention to petty petitions, such as for supporting one's favorite team in a football match, finding a parking spot, or, harder still, imbuing those attending a meeting with wisdom? And if God does not answer the pleas of the many in extreme situations like 9/11 or the 2004 tsunami, why should God be expected to answer those with minor requests, even legitimate individual ones like dealing with the suffering of AIDS or cancer?

Other peoples and faiths have endured catastrophes of their own. Then too, each of us must wrestle with the suffering, pain, and death that make life such a challenging experience. Many people, like Iyov, have feelings of anger and abandonment; many question the absence of God's saving presence or protest against God's perceived indifference to their fates. I think that the reason many Jews today do not attend synagogue very much for worship purposes is, in part, due to the cognitive dissonance between the traditional prayers, which build on the Exodus experience, and personal or recent historical experiences of suffering. Perhaps the large numbers of religiously unaffiliated people in America, and people exploring alternative religious traditions, and, paradoxically, the numbers of people turning to more "fundamentalist" forms of faith indicate that the problem isn't confined to the Jewish people alone.[1]

A second part of my problem with traditional prayer has to do with how we Jews pray. To be a Jew—or a member of any group, I suppose—is to wrestle with one's inherited traditions. On the one hand, I am not a free-floating individual—I am one contemporary link in a 3,500-year-old chain and I don't want my people and its faith to end with me. On the other hand, precisely because I am a member of an ancient people, I *do* carry a lot of religious baggage, and not all of it is wonderful or great.[2] Generally speaking, I think Jews do to themselves in prayer what the Japanese do to trees in bonsai: we prune our natural spiritual inclinations to fit a prescribed shape. We practice the art of spiritual bonsai in order to accommodate ourselves to conform to the traditional modes of prayer and the traditional concepts of God. I'm sure we're not unique in this practice. I think it is what many religions do with basic human spirituality.[3]

I have great respect for people of any faith who can invest an ancient liturgy with the yearnings of their souls, who can still relate to a personal, supernatural God; and I salute those clergy who strive to make

---

1. See, for example, Bass, *Grounded*.

2. When Helen Vandeman, author of *We Are One*, read a draft of this book, she commented:

> I am so grateful I don't have to *unlearn* a religious teaching to understand or know! What I got very clearly upon reading your MS is your issues are not about or w/God, but about how God is portrayed in the Torah, and therefore, in Judaism. Therefore, it is about Anson arguing with his history/path/past/ Judaism, etc.

She was so right, but, to quote someone famous: "I am who I am."

3. I think there is a great fear in some quarters about unbridled spiritual expression. There always has been. For one thing, it threatens those with the power and authority to determine what proper orthodox behavior is and what is not. It can undermine belief, lead people down strange unauthorized paths. Imagine the kinds of prayers people might have offered—the things they might have said to God—if allowed, immediately after the Holocaust. Imagine what individuals might say in the depths of suffering from illness or grief. Imagine the myriad of different ways of prayer and forms of ritual and ideas that might exist today if people's spirituality had been less restricted by religious authorities over the centuries. Far better to keep things under tight control so that our world—and our concepts of God—are not unduly disturbed. In these ways liturgies are harmful. But liturgies are also beneficial. They affirm common beliefs, shared praise, and sanctioned requests. They confirm the group identity. They assert values and sustain hope. And all that really is fine by me—after all, I *am* a rabbi, nearly as much invested in preserving my people's traditions as I am in stirring up their spiritual struggles.

the traditional prayers more relevant to contemporary congregations. For me, however, more often than not, the ancient words just get in the way, although singing them in Hebrew makes the prayers easier to swallow, just the way (as the song says) that a spoonful of sugar helps the medicine go down, because singing engages a different part of the brain and heart. But I have to ask myself: "Why go to such lengths to provide meaning to words that no longer fit our times? Why not create something new, something that works for us today?"

A third component of my problem with prayer has to do with how prayer is expressed: On some level, I consider prayer—any sort of articulated prayer—to be like blasphemy because it limits and constrains God, either by whatever words we can fathom to use or because of the expectations prayers put on God. During the time when the ancient rabbis were institutionalizing the Jewish liturgy, at least some also recognized the absurdity of trying to use human language to praise a being as mysterious and ineffable as God. In one talmudic story, a man improvised on the traditional prayers by adding to God's praise as follows: "the great, the mighty the awesome, the glorious, the powerful, the valiant, the fearless, the strong, the sure, and the honored." Rabbi Hanina waited patiently until he finished and then said to him: "Are you all through? Why did you stop when you did? Did you finish all the praises of God? Why all these extra words? Even the three words of praise we do say, if Moshe [Moses] had not mentioned them in the Torah . . . we would not be allowed to recite even these three. Yet you say all this and keep going on and on!"[4] On the one hand, it boggles the mind to imagine trying to communicate with an essentially ineffable Presence but, on the other hand, there has hardly been a society in human history that has not assumed the ability to interact with the divine in some way. This remains a basic desire for many people.

Lastly, I have a serious problem with the limited tone of prayer. In most faith traditions, public prayer is limited to praise, petition, penitence, and thanksgiving. But how do you pray to God with all the hostile feelings that accompany the experience of suffering? In a troubled human relationship, negative feelings are communicated, more or less effectively, to the other person involved. But when the other party is God, then the form of communication is called "prayer" and, in many traditions, including the normative Jewish one, prayers that give voice to negative sentiments would be considered impious or even blasphemous. Anger and protest and

4. *b. Berachot* 33b.

lamenting are not considered appropriate in tone for addressing "our Father in heaven." So how does one pray when bad things happen to basically good people? How do you pray the intense feelings that go with that?

II PRAYER AS PROTEST

As we saw in chapter 1, the book of Iyov challenged the dominant theodicy of its day in part by Iyov's fiery prayers of protest. This response to suffering, which I call "arguing with God," endeavors to hold fast to both ends of the "Exodus"/"experience" contradiction by calling God to account. Never mind that one party is the Creator, God Almighty, and the other is God's creation, a creature of dust and ashes. The two are bound together by a covenant (*breet*, in Hebrew), which is basically a contract or agreement, a rather unique way of framing the divine-human relationship.

Because of the Covenant, both the Jewish people and God have the right to take the other party to task if said party is not fulfilling the terms of the Covenant and demand change. This rather odd assumption—that one could compel God to change behavior—was based on the idea that even God had to adhere to the covenantal principle of justice. It is first clearly articulated in the story of Avraham challenging God about the proposed annihilation of *S'dom* (Sodom) and *Amorah* (Gomorrah) when Avraham declares: "Will you sweep away the innocent along with the guilty . . . Far be it from you to do such a thing . . . Shall not the judge of all the earth deal justly?"[5] The question was not necessarily rhetorical and the divine answer could have been anything, however, by bargaining with Avraham over the cities' fate, God confirmed Avraham's statement that justice rules supreme, even over God. At the same time, the conclusion of this episode demonstrates another key principle of the Jewish covenantal worldview, namely, that of divine mercy.[6]

In the "arguing with God" stance, when bad things happened, God might simultaneously be praised for the events of the Exodus and reproached for failing to intervene in the tragedy of the day. In this way, the

5. Ber/Gen 18:23–25.

6. See Ber/Gen 18:17—19:29. Avraham had challenged God to do justly and God agreed to spare the cities if ten righteous people could be found there. When less than ten were found, God nonetheless mercifully spared Lot and his family from sharing the fate of the citizens of S'dom although, according to the agreement with Avraham, God could have annihilated them along with everyone else.

people's expectation to see God's ultimate justice was affirmed, but their feelings of anger and abandonment also were articulated in prayers of protest. It is a tradition that started with the Avraham story cited above and continues down to our own day.

Consider the following examples:

In *Tehilla (Psalm)* 44, God's great acts in the past are celebrated: "We have heard with our ears, O God, our ancestors have told us what deeds you performed in their time, in the days of old." But then just a few stanzas later come harsh accusations:

> Yet you have rejected and disgraced us . . .
>
> You let them devour us like sheep;
>
> You disperse us among the nations . . .
>
> All this has come upon us,
>
> yet we have not forgotten you
>
> or been false to your covenant . . .
>
> Rouse yourself; why do you sleep, O Lord? . . .
>
> Why do you hide your face,
>
> ignoring our affliction and distress?
>
> Arise and help us,
>
> redeem us, as befits your faithfulness.

Words like these are both a protest *and* an argument, or at least one side of an argument. God's apparent inactivity is questioned but God's power and authority are not, because the expectation is that God will respond, that God will answer their protest with action, just as in the case of Iyov.

Jewish suffering over the centuries has made a case for a sustained argument with God, often based on the Exodus precedent. Centuries later, in rabbinic stories (midrash) dealing with the destruction of the Second Temple and the oppression in Roman times, the rabbis set the following prayer in the mouth of their character, a personified Yisrael:

> Master of the Universe! You did wonders for our ancestors, will you not do them for us? . . . What a work you performed in bringing them forth out of Egypt and dividing the sea for them! But you have not done anything like that for us! . . . You did it for them, but not for us . . . When will you work a good sign for us? . . . "Show us your mercy, O Lord, and grant us your salvation."[7]

---

7. *Midrash Tehillim* 44:1.

This being midrash, God responds: "Indeed I shall be favorable to you also," and Tehilla/Psalm 85:2 is cited as proof of God's intentions in the future to restore Yisrael to its land. Anger, complaint, a plea, and a word of divine comfort—it was a good message for the people to hear in those difficult, trying times.

Centuries later, during the time of the Crusader massacres in Europe, rabbi-poets wrote poem-prayers called *piyyutim*, and many of these continued this quarrel with God. In one of these prayers of protest, the author plays savagely on the words of Shemot/Exodus 15:11: "Who is like you among the mighty [*elim*], Lord?" But he adds one letter, a *mem* מ, to the word *elim* so it becomes *elmim*, with the result that the verse now reads: "Who is like you among the dumb, Lord!"

> Who is like you among the dumb, my God?
>
> You kept silence.
>
> You were silent when they destroyed your Temple.
>
> You remained silent when the wicked trod your children underfoot . . .
>
> We came through fire, water and flame.
>
> They mastered us, stoned us, and hung us on scaffolds.
>
> They rode on our heads, but we declared our love for you.
>
> We descended into Sheol while living and we were swallowed . . .
>
> You are the zealous one and avenger,
>
> where then is your vengeance?[8]

This poem-prayer is all the more audacious because it plays most seriously on the opening line of a major prayer in the Jewish liturgy that celebrates God's miraculous intervention at the Sea of Reeds.

Another poem, written during the terrible Khmelnytsky (or Chmielnicki) pogroms in seventeenth-century Ukraine, demanded: "When will the day of the final miracles come? Your sons and your daughters are given into the hands of an alien nation and your eyes see! Show us your miracles as during our exodus from Egypt!"[9]

---

8. Menachem ben Yaakov (d. 1203), "Woe unto me," quoted in Zinberg, *Jewish Literature*, 2:26. For full text in Hebrew, see Bernfeld, *Sefer Hadema'ot*, 1:239–40. A similar poem, "There Is None Like You among the Dumb," by Yitzhak bar Shalom, whose first line plays on Teh/Ps 86:8, can be found in Hebrew and English, with notes and commentary, in Petuchowski, *Theology and Poetry*, 74–80. Both poets base their blasphemy on a teaching of the school of Rabbi Yishmael, found in *b. Gittin* 56b.

9. Gavriel ben Yehoshua Strassberg of Raisha (seventeenth century), "How Can I Lift My Face?," quoted in Dubnow, *History of the Jews*, 4:48. For full text in Hebrew, see

And even now, in our post-Holocaust era, the Jewish quarrel with God continues, although today it is our poets and authors, not rabbis, who continue the tradition. Consider this poem by Friedrich Torberg, an Austrian Jew who made it to America in 1940, regarding the Passover seder:

> Lord, I am not one of the just.
> Don't ask me, Lord, for I could not answer.
> I do not know, you see, why for your servants here
> this night is so different
> from all the others. Why?
>
> The youngest child was happy once
> to learn the answer at the table feast:
> Because we were slaves in Egypt,
> in bondage to wicked Pharaoh
> thousands of years ago.
>
> And because, O Lord, you led us forth
> with an outstretched arm
> and delivered us from oppression and grief
> and treacheries numbering a thousand,
> we sit, reclining, and break into crumpling pieces
> our fathers' bread of affliction . . .
>
> And so we give thee thanks, O Lord,
> for saving us from harm,
> as we gather believing
> today, and here, and in every land,
> and "next year in Jerusalem."
>
> The youngest child who heard all this
> has long since lost his faith.
> The answer of old no longer holds,
> for "next year" never came, O Lord,
> and the night weighs down heavy and dark.
>
> We still have not wandered across the sand.

Bernfeld, *Sefer Hadema'ot*, 3:179–81.

we still have not seen the Promised Land,
we still have not eaten the bread of the free,
we still have not done with the bitter herbs.

For time and again in our weary wanderings
Pharaoh has set upon our trail,
behind us he comes with his bloody henchmen—
the carts, O Lord, do you hear their clatter—
O Lord, where have you led us to!

You sent us on without a star,
we stand at the shore and stare on high,
O Lord, the flood has not returned,
O Lord, the night is not yet past,
"Why is this night so different from . . ."[10]

Prayers of protest such as these, while perhaps sounding blasphemous to our ears, were all backhanded ways of affirming the belief in God's ultimate justice and mercy, just as surely as the normative prayers did. Once the protest was lodged, it was assumed that, at some point in the future, God would make things right. The point is that *if* God had not saved Israel from Egyptian bondage, *then* there would be no expectation that God would save the Children of Yisrael again. But, since it is traditionally believed that God *did* save the Children of Yisrael in Egypt—that God *does* watch over humanity and that God *does* intervene in human life—then, when experience contradicted expectation, prayers of protest were one response that the people and their spiritual leaders chose to utilize to voice their anguish.

But prayers of protest were not always angry. In the eighteenth century, some Jews of Eastern Europe sought a new way to cope with tragedy and created Hasidism, which sought to minimize suffering by focusing on the immediacy of prayer, the presence of God in all things, and the need to live joyfully. The Hasidic *rebbes* (masters) presumed a personal and intimate relationship with God and encouraged their followers to have the

10. Friedrich Torberg, "Seder, 1944," in Schwartz and Rudolf, *Voices within the Ark*, 980–81. Torberg's "blasphemy" is mild compared to other post-Holocaust poets. Consider this short prayer by Perets Markish, part of a much longer poem called *The Mound*, written response to Ukrainian pogroms of 1919–20: "I yearn to merge with you in prayer / And yet my heart, my lips are moved / Only to blasphemies and curses." In Howe et al., *Penguin Book of Modern Yiddish Verse*, 358.

same. Protest was part of that relationship with God but, unlike earlier arguments, Hasidic arguments often were gentler, more loving, and even humorous. Laughter has always been a great narcotic palliative for suffering. Often even their protests to God often had a lighter tone even though the content was as painfully felt as in prior generations. Consider this story about the great Hasidic master Levi Yitzhak of Berditchev and a simple tailor:

> On one Yom Kippur, the Rabbi interrupted services to call up a simple tailor before the entire congregation. He asked him to relate his argument with God from the previous day.
>
> The tailor replied: "I declared: 'Dear God, You want me to repent of my sins during the past year, but I have committed only minor offenses: I may have kept leftover cloth instead of giving it to my customers, or I may have eaten in a non-Jewish home, where I worked, without washing my hands. But You, dear God, have committed grievous sins: You have taken away babies from their mothers, and mothers from their babies. But I'll make a deal with You: You forgive my sins and I will forgive Yours!'"
>
> Said the Rabbi, shaking his head: "Why did you let God off so easily? You could have forced Him (to send the Messiah) to redeem all of Israel . . ."[11]

When I think about the Jewish tradition of praying prayers of protest, I reflect that the tailor's quarrel with God took place in the context of an accepting community and an accepting faith. After all, the tailor's rabbi asked him to repeat his prayer before the entire congregation on the holiest day of the year, no less—and then chided him for not striking a harder bargain. We relate to God both as individuals and in community; a good argument with God needs communal witnesses and the endorsement of a community leader to provide moral support to the protester.

The experience of suffering, whether personal and collective, is traumatic and the pain must be articulated if any healing is to occur. Today, if we truly want to be honest, not only to God and the biblical accounts, but also to our own experience, then we should try expressing our anger with God when we gather to pray in response to tragedies and/or when we gather to mourn and grieve over loved ones. If we believe that God is the Creator and Preserver of all, then doing this might be efficacious—if not

11. Quoted in Newman, *Hasidic Anthology*, 57.

to rouse God to action, then at least for people in emotional and spiritual pain.

In addition, for those people familiar with these prayers of protest, whether the psalms of lament or later works, partaking of this mode introduces them to the unusual but potentially helpful theological motif of a God who seems absent yet whose presence is sought; a God who appears to be silent yet whose voice is longed to be heard; a God who is seen as passive yet whose activity is demanded. All these can play a role in shaping the contemporary relationship with God.

For decades, beginning in the 1970s,[12] I "argued with God." It is encouraging to see that in recent years the "arguing with God" approach has gained currency in segments of both the Jewish and Christian worlds and has also seen potential application to a broad variety of situations. David Blumenthal, in *Facing the Abusing God: A Theology of Protest*, utilizes the accounts of both survivors of child sexual abuse and of the Holocaust to make the case for prayers of protest against an often abusive God. Dov Weiss has explored the rabbinic roots of confronting God in a wonderfully detailed scholarly book,[13] while Shmuley Boteach uses the tradition of "arguing with God" in an attempt to reconcile suffering with traditional Judaism and its view of God.[14] Kathleen Billman and Daniel Migliore, and John Swinton, explore the pastoral and spiritual dimensions of the lament if it were to be adopted as part of Christian usage.[15] William Morrow, in *Protest against God: The Eclipse of a Biblical Tradition*, believes ours is an age that will see a revival of prayers of protest in Jewish worship—and for the first time in Christian prayer too.[16] More recently, Peter Admirand, in

12. Morrow, *Protest Against God*, 3 nn. 8–10, notes that Claus Westermann and Walter Brueggemann began their pioneering work in this field as it pertained to biblical studies in the 1970s—precisely when I also began my research into this subject as a young rabbinical student.

13. Weiss, *Pious Irreverence*.

14. Boteach, *Wrestling with the Divine*.

15. Billman and Migliore, *Rachel's Cry*. Swinton, *Raging with Compassion*. Morrow, *Protest Against God*, 214 n. 32, references a number of Christian works dealing with the pastoral possibilities for addressing individual suffering through psalms of individual lament.

16. Morrow, *Protest Against God*. Unique in Christian tradition, African-American spirituality apparently also protested against God. Morrow cites David E. Goatley's *Were You There?: Godforsakeness in Slave Religion* for the tradition of complaint against God among Afro-American slaves (210, n 20) and Langston Hughes, in his story "Cora Unashamed," has the title character "cuss out" God when her baby dies, in Harper, ed.,

Amidst Mass Atrocity and the Rubble of Theology: Searching for a Viable Theodicy, has taken the need for a protest against divine apathy global, given the ubiquitous nature of human suffering. For people still wrestling with a traditional, supernatural God, these developments are all for the better because, by advocating for the inclusion of prayers of protest, they make a relationship with that kind of God more honest and more complete.

Although I am no longer in my "arguing with God" phase of spirituality, I still believe that people should be encouraged to express their feelings of anger, betrayal, abandonment, and injustice; that they shouldn't sit on their feelings and pretend that nothing bad has happened and that all is well between them and God. I believed then—and still believe—that there is a need, and there should be a place, for individual and collective prayers of protest and anger because prayer should reflect the reality of experience and God—whatever God is—is big enough and tough enough to be able to handle honest communication from the likes of us.[17] It is both theologically and psychologically sound.

Langston Hughes Short Stories, 43.

17. My colleague in the "prayer of protest" school David Blumenthal maintains a much more traditional relationship with the "Jewish" God, despite the fact that he considers God to be abusive. He continues to pray as tradition requires and he suggests that we ought to love our God, warts and all, regardless of God's faults and failings. In an email to me Blumenthal wrote:

> I personally do not have any problem protesting, praising, or petitioning. To address God is to address God—in several modes. Just because God does not . . . answer us with dispatch, does not mean we do not ask. I try not to ask for silly things but there are a few really serious items on my list: health, a job for my kids, a sense of my own sanity, the reality of God's presence, plus the national issue of peace, etc.
>
> I don't think you and I are addressing our own God-concepts. That might be easier than what we do do—address the God of the tradition, Who is active, concerned, and responsive. I'm not sure either of us would invent such a God. But, given that God, we are doing our best to stay in the game, to stay present to that God—in praise which is not so hard, in petition which is harder, and in protest which is hardest.
>
> It's all not unlike maintaining human relationships. I work at that and, when all is said and done, I try to be present to others . . . It is not easy. Buber used to say that the hardest part about being a human being was being as fully present as one can to the other.

III THE ONE TIME I ACTUALLY OFFERED A PERSONAL PRAYER OF PROTEST

In 1999, my sister-in-law, Jane, died quickly, tragically, and far too young of a brain tumor. At the same time, my wife, Merrily, was struggling to cope with ovarian cancer. We all were emotionally devastated so, rather than conducting the funeral service myself, I asked a rabbinical colleague to do it. Instead, I decided to offer a reflection/prayer for those of us—myself, family members, and friends—who had trouble accepting what had happened and who could not in good conscience utter the compliant, pious words required of us by the traditional Jewish funeral liturgy. It was my intention to speak honestly about things but, even more importantly, I also hoped my words would be therapeutic or pastoral, meant to begin moving us from anger toward acceptance.

I started off by quoting the most troubling lines from the Jewish funeral service:

> The Rock, his work is perfect; for all his ways are just; a God of faithfulness and without iniquity. The Rock, perfect in all his deeds: Who dares say, "What is it that you do?" to him who rules above and below, who takes away life and gives it, who brings down to the grave and raises up. Righteous are you, Adonai, in taking away or giving life, for in your hand are pledged all spirits. We know, Adonai, that your judgments are right, your decrees just, and your rulings pure. None should presume to question your judgments. Praised be the True Judge.

Then I interjected:

> But we *do* question; we *do* protest! *Ribbono Shel Olam*, Ruler of the World, I call you to task for breaking two of your own Commandments.
>
> You have murdered *and* you have stolen. With this cancer, part of your creation, You have murdered first Michael, and now Jane, cut them down in the prime of their lives. With it, you also threaten the life of their sister, Merrily. And, as if this were not enough, you have stolen. You have stolen precious years that ought to have belonged to Jane. You have stolen years of love and companionship from her, from her husband, from her mother, from her sister, from her children, from her beloved grandchildren, and from her many friends and colleagues. Dear God, it is intolerable what you put us through sometimes!

And yet, what choice do we have? Whatever happens, happens. There is no way to avoid this truth of existence. Is it preferable to ascribe all things to God's will as our tradition holds, or is it better to call life a random series of events and experiences, without sense or order? That is for each of us to determine for ourselves.

In the end, we can only accept what happens, whether we believe it comes from God or not. There is no choice but to accept. Even in this case, even with our Jane. We can only accept and continue on, dealing with our feelings of loss and grief as best we can.

So, dear God, although we must accept what has happened, and what happens everyday all around us, that does not mean that we accept it as your will. We cannot, we will not, offer words of praise to you if indeed this was your deed.

But we can offer thanks for the very existence of this wonderful woman, for how Jane touched our many lives in so many different ways: as child, sister, wife, mother, in-law, grandmother, friend, colleague, and therapist. Though her life was too short by half, she lived it passionately, intensely, and we are all better for having had her as a portion of our own life experiences. Her life was indeed a blessing to us all.

For having known her, and for having loved her, and for having been loved by her, we gather now both to honor her memory and praise your holy Name. Amen.

This was the only occasion on which I have been brave enough to actually "argue with God." I was not struck down for my *chutzpah*. My anger was my own and my heart was pure in its prayer of protest. While I spoke it, no one uttered a sound and after the burial service many people came up to thank me for articulating what had been lurking unspoken in their hearts.

IV THE FUTURE OF PRAYER

I think that the need to "pray" is almost innate. Perhaps, as Nicholas Wade has suggested, we are born with a faith instinct.[18] Certainly I have seen it firsthand in my children and grandchildren as they try to puzzle out life, death, and things beyond. It is as if they each discover God independently and then seek confirmation from the adults in their lives (who at that point

---

18. See Wade, *Faith Instinct*. "Faith," for Wade and for me, does not mean belief. We use it as a synonym for religion.

probably will provide religious education/indoctrination rather than engaging in the spiritual discussion that is called for).

Humankind has always wanted to express thanks or beg for favors, and prayer and ritual are part of many religions. Religions may evolve or vanish, but people will continually reach for something transcendent beyond their mortal existence, seeking a sense of connection or comfort or something else yet again that will help inform their finite lives with meaning and support. That, I think, is the primary purpose of prayer and ritual: it's about developing a relationship with the divine, however understood. In their purest form, prayer and ritual are about connecting with the divine, i.e., offering the opportunity to have a spiritual experience. Therefore, everything else—all the words of praise, petition, penitence, and even protest—is secondary.

So ritual and prayer, by which I mean our efforts to relate to and connect with God, are here to stay. Even so, I predict that they will change radically. Two thousand years ago, animal sacrifices were the dominant form of worship around the world. Eventually, in many cultures, sacrifices were replaced by rituals of prayer and song.[19] During this same period, our various conceptions of God also changed, although not necessarily with our awareness of our having done so. Today, when many of us look at the idea of offering animal sacrifices to God, we are likely to exclaim: "What were these people thinking? Did they really believe God wanted *that*?!" Similarly, I think that in the future our way of relating to God will be as dramatically different from worship as practiced today as today's practice of prayer and ritual is from when sacrifices were the dominant mode of worship. Some day people may look at the prayers we've been using for the past several millennia—all those words of praise, self-abasement, or dogmatic assertion—and bemusedly ask themselves: "What were these people thinking? Did they really believe God wanted *that*?!"

After my year as an interim congregational rabbi, where one of my major tasks was to serve as the communal prayer leader, I feel more certain

19. My mentor and friend Jordan Paper reminds me that Judaism never ended ritual slaughter because, to be kosher, an animal must be killed by a ritual butcher. Jews also traditionally pray for the return of the sacrificial cult in the rebuilt Temple. Paper also noted that at the birthday ritual sacrifice to Kongzi (Confucius) in Taipei, following the ritual going back over a couple of thousand years, a sacrificed goat, pig, and cow are splayed out on a frame as the primary offering; and in Hinduism many thousands of goats are sacrificed to Kali once a year; while in many Native American traditions, for the gift of life one offers in recompense life fluid—one's own blood or pieces of flesh.

than ever that ritualized prayer as we Jews do it belongs to an era of the past. This is not to say that the ancient prayers do not speak to people—and even to me—still. These prayers ask of God what people seek for themselves: health, sustenance, understanding, forgiveness, contentment, peace. They also affirm the values that people cherish: trustworthiness, gratitude, slowness to anger, forgiveness, compassion, justice, love, and love of peace. They just project these desires outwardly, as petitions or as praise, to God in heaven. Other prayers offer collective affirmation of key beliefs.

But here's the rub: what to replace traditional prayer rituals with? Prayer rituals are unlike any other activity in that they able to imbue diverse individual human beings with a sense of community and simultaneously connect that community with the divine and with their ancestors in a way that touches both head and heart. What other activity can do all that?

In the future, I think that ritual will continue because ritual is as basic to our nature as the "faith instinct." We humans love rituals; we use them everywhere to mark all kinds of occasions, both religious and secular, and events frivolous or serious. So ritual—ancient or modern, traditional or creative—will continue in some form. Prayer, as we know it in the Abrahamic faiths, will continue as well but our way of praying will change in accordance with our changing ideas about God. I think prayer will embrace expressions of gratitude and allow for feelings of anger; it will involve silence and meditation, and song and praise; and it will include the opportunity for personal reflection and transformation. Prayers for healing and comfort will be offered, not in the sense of alerting God to the need for intervention, but to make the community aware of its members' needs for support. And I know that music will play a key role because music taps into a different part of our brains; it can reach into our souls and touch us in a different way than merely reading words aloud does.

Accompanied by appropriate rituals and music, prayer in the future will be comprised of three main components: contemplation, personal transformation, and gratitude.[20]

20. There is a fourth component as well, at least in Judaism, where many prayers instruct the worshiper in the essential tenets of the faith. This sort of prayer will continue as well, changing as the beliefs change. A good example of this is how Reform Judaism has dealt with—and continues to deal with—prayers regarding "chosenness."

Contemplation

A friend, Andrew Fenniman, pointed out that I was viewing prayer only as liturgy. "What about Quaker-style prayer?," he asked. "Not only do they contemplate silently; they don't speak unless the Spirit moves them. There are many ways to pray." True indeed and his comment reminds me that as far as I know there is a contemplative form of prayer in many religions.

In a famous Hasidic story, an illiterate boy's blowing of his flute on Yom Kippur as prayer (a big no-no) meant more to God than did the beautifully articulated prayers of the entire congregation. It is not the words that matter; it is the intention (*kavana*) alone that really counts. The Talmud tells us that what God requires of us in prayer is the heart.[21] Regardless of the forms of prayer we utilize, "the heart"—intentionality—is what must be cultivated and it is a highly personal endeavor.

The contemplative traditions all offer an old/new way of connecting with the divine that is different than our normative way of praying. My wife, Richelle, a practitioner of yoga and meditation for many years, would advocate for her form of practice as an alternative to traditional prayer, and Fr. Thomas Keating's "centering prayer" movement is a contemporary contemplative form of Christian prayer. Rabbis Ted Falcon, Yoel Glick, the late Alan Lew and others have tapped into the various forms of meditation and the Jewish mystical tradition to revive Jewish meditation as a form of worship. All these developments are necessary correctives to our society's overemphasis on collective prayer at the expense of individual experience. They enable us to cultivate our intentionality in order to connect with the divine and to achieve inner balance. The challenge as I see it is how to build a sense of community and collective purpose from an activity (or a form of prayer) that is essentially a uniquely personal and individualistic experience. The challenge doesn't obviate the value of contemplation, it just complicates its application in congregational settings. (This problem I happily leave to others to work out.)

Personal Transformation

There *is* a type of prayer I find appealing because its focus is on changing the attitude of the one who prays rather than asking God to intervene in

21. *b. Sanhedrin* 106b.

some way. I call it transformational or reflexive prayer.[22] Unlike praying, "God give me the wisdom to deal with this issue," this form of prayer is self-directed: "May I find within me the wisdom to deal with this issue." Reflexive prayer makes sense to me because it aims to transform the person making it.

A colleague at Multifaith Works, Ed Shields, formerly a Catholic priest, used to think that prayer was "begging God to do something or give something" but, over many years, has gradually shifted his perspective. This is how the now-internalized process of reflexive prayer works for him:

> More and more, I see prayer as changing me or putting me in line with God's thinking. I express my feelings honestly to God. Then I look at how I might respond to the issue that troubles me . . . Then I realize hopefully that this issue or event is an opportunity to respond with compassion and with love. My prayer then moves me and not God. This is not an easy or always successful process, but I am working at it. Often it takes some time to arrive at my being changed or moved.[23]

Rachel Naomi Remen, in her book *Kitchen Table Wisdom: Stories That Heal*, enlarges on this reflexive prayer process:

> I think that prayer may be less about asking for things we are attached to than it is about relinquishing our attachments in some way . . . When we pray, we don't change the world, we change ourselves. We change our consciousness. We move from an individual, isolated making-things-happen kind of consciousness to a connection on the deepest level with the largest possible reality . . . When we pray, we stop trying to control life and remember that we belong to life. It is an opportunity to experience humility and recognize grace.[24]

According to the ancient rabbis, even God uses the reflexive form of prayer. Consider "God's own personal prayer" as imagined by the rabbis:

> May it be my will that my compassion may overcome my anger, and that it may prevail over my attributes of justice and judgment,

---

22. I find it ironic that, while so much of Jewish prayer is non-reflexive and directed to a supernatural God, the Hebrew word for "to pray" is *hitpalel*, a reflexive verb meaning in its root "to judge oneself." To me, this is indicative that, at its core, Jewish prayer was supposed to be personal and self-transformative rather than externally focused.

23. Email.

24. Remen, *Kitchen Table Wisdom*, 270–71.

and that I may deal with my children according to the attribute of compassion, and that I may not act towards them according to the strict line of justice.[25]

As much as it may help God, this is also a prayer I use regularly in my own life to encourage my better inclinations.

Like a traditional prayer that would ask for God's help, transformational prayers enable you to focus on your needs, to center your energy and intention, and to find hope, but without raising the expectation that God will respond by intervening directly. What we ask for, hope for, and expect of God when we offer petitionary prayers is what we really need from ourselves and one another: trust, compassion, justice, mercy, love, forgiveness, saving acts, peace-making and so on. Reflexive prayers can help us to focus on, celebrate, and actualize those values that we hold most dear. They allow us to focus on the power for good that resides within each of us in order to bring it out in its fullest possible expression in the world. Like traditional prayer, it builds hope for a better future.[26] What matters is that whatever kind of prayer you do should help you learn to stay centered and to be able to transcend whatever happens in life and to adapt in response to those experiences. The key is an attitudinal shift and that is what these reflexive prayers consciously seek to accomplish.

Gratitude / Wonder

Thankfulness remains for me something worth praying about, regardless of how one views God. Albert Einstein once said that there are two ways

25. *b. Berachot* 7a.

26. A friend of mine, Charles Davis, wrote:

> Petitionary prayer is based on hope. Hope, said George Bernard Shaw, is the triumph of faith over experience. Your "Holocaust test" says the lesson of experience is that hope, when expressed as prayer, is not justified. But isn't hope, even when not explicitly expressed as prayer, always a form of prayer? And if hope is not justified—if there is no hope—why continue to live? I have long thought that there are only two reasons we get out of bed in the morning: to go to the bathroom and because we are optimists.

He was right to call me on this point. Even though I cannot in good conscience offer petitionary prayers, nonetheless I *do* continue to have hope. I continue to have hope in my fellow human beings and even in God—despite the fact that, after the Holocaust, hope in neither of these really seems warranted. I have hope; but I am not particularly optimistic. I am a realist who would love to be surprised.

of going through life: one is as though nothing is a miracle; the other is as though everything is a miracle. It all depends on attitude. I choose to look at life as a miracle and gratitude is my response—even when things seem bad. For example, my attachment to my late wife and my grief over the loss of our future together caused me much pain and suffering. But that same attachment—the love we shared and the life we built together for ourselves and our family—is also a reason for profound and abiding gratitude. I am grateful despite my ongoing grief and sadness.

Traditionally, when we give thanks or praise to God, ideally speaking, it means that we are consciously articulating an inner awareness of the manifold gifts we receive from the Creator of all. A wholly holy person would not be someone with an episodic sense of wonder; s/he would have a consciousness of a divine connection and an attitude of radical gratitude every minute of every day. (That may be what being enlightened is all about.)

However, recognizing that most human beings are unable to attain or maintain this exalted state, the rabbis of yore sought to elevate people's souls at least occasionally. They decreed, for example, that a person ought to recite at least one hundred blessings each day: for waking from sleep, for the working of our bodies, for our ability to perform God's will, for the gift of Torah and its commandments, for the food we eat and the clothes we wear, for life itself and whatever it may bring. These "gratitudes," as I call them, are an example of everyday mysticism, an opportunity to develop a deeper spiritual awareness in daily life.

While I struggle with the inadequacy of words to express feelings to and about God, I am truly aware of the gift of life and of the unique potentiality it holds, despite all my family has gone through. You cannot work with people living with AIDS, as I did, or go through too many too-close encounters with death, as our family has, without it sharpening your appreciation of the true fragility of life, and wonder at its unique preciousness and value. Once touched by suffering and death, you never forget and you are never the same.

But you don't need a brush with mortality to be reminded of the miracle of life and of life's opportunities. This can be had every moment of every day. There is a Jewish prayer that traditionally is said upon arising each day: "I am grateful to you, living and enduring God, for restoring my soul to me in compassion. Great is your faithfulness." Prayers such as this one still work for me on some level because they help me maintain "right attitude" and "right perspective." This prayer reminds me of the fact that whatever I enjoy in life begins simply and most mysteriously with the life to which I awaken each and every morning so far.[27]

Another example: We don't talk about bodily functions in polite society. In fact, there are only two occasions when discussion of bodily functions is really socially acceptable: when there is a baby present or when someone is sick. But the way our bodies work is as much a miracle as anything else.

And so it was that when my late wife was recuperating from her abdominal surgery that the first words out of the surgeon's mouth to her were: "Got gas?"

"How rude!" is what I immediately thought. And I made a joke about it.

But then the surgeon explained. "Gas is good," she said. "Gas is a sign of vitality. If we don't produce gas in our intestines we are in big trouble because it means our bowels aren't working as they should." (Descartes should have said: "I fart, therefore I am.")

Working with people living with AIDS makes one aware of the importance of nitty-gritty things like gas and bowels. We all share their concerns, although not perhaps with the same intensity, but how important these things are! If our bowel movements are too frequent, we complain; if they're too infrequent, we complain. If they don't happen at all or if they happen all the time, we die. The human body is a finely balanced mechanism. When problems occur, it is the little things that matter; so for the smooth operation of our bodies we should be grateful regularly.

In Jewish custom, there is prayer that thanks God for making our bodies work the way they do, which is said after going to the toilet.[28] Perhaps

---

27. David Steindl-Rast once wrote to me:

> There is life-affirming suffering, like birth pangs, and life-denying suffering like torture. I do not know where this evil suffering has its origin, but I do know that God does not intend it. We need a new image of God as not controlling by external power, but guiding everything from within, giving meaning even to the pain we suffer, transforming it and making it life-giving when it is borne in love . . . One benefit of suffering is that it challenges us to go forward in this process. In this sense it is growing pain. And for growing we can be grateful.

28. "Praised are you, YHVH our God, Ruler of the universe, who has formed human beings in wisdom, and created in them many openings and vessels. It is well known before your glorious throne that if but one of these doesn't work properly, it would be impossible to exist and stand before you. Praised are you, YHVH, healer of all flesh, who

it seems odd to you, or perhaps not, to thank God for having formed our bodies with the ability to work as they do, but to pass gas, to have a bowel movement, etc. are as much miracles of Creation as is a mountain vista or a spectacular sunset, would that we were uninhibited enough to be willing to acknowledge them as such. Gratitude is what is called for.

Personally, I look for ways to express gratitude regardless of what I happen to encounter in life. When things were at their darkest in my life— as when, on the first anniversary of my father's still-too-sudden death, I was told that my wife had to have emergency abdominal surgery, while our daughter was lying in another hospital trying to cope with the aftereffects of chemotherapy for her leukemia; or even more, as my wife lay dying ten years later—I could still find a thing or two for which to be grateful: for love, for life itself, for time spent together. I was grateful even though I cried with stress and incredible grief. Gratefulness does not necessarily mean happiness. I find it in tears as well as in smiles. Radical gratefulness is a matter of right mindfulness—staying in the here and now, focusing, and being aware. I, however, find it simply impossible to remain continually aware of the exquisitely painful/wondrous impermanence of existence and I cannot begin to appreciate Creation and life enough, let alone to express what I feel.[29]

The key thing for me is to try to maintain this sense of radical gratefulness as I go about my daily routines. When I remember to try, I can uncover a sense of radical wonder and a corresponding need to express radical gratefulness for just about everything, regardless of my situation—even if I don't use the traditional blessings to acknowledge it.[30] But, in truth, despite my best efforts, I often take far too much for granted. In order to help me stay focused and aware, I went through a period when I took to muttering an ancient Jewish blessing, one that traditionally is used just on holidays, special occasions, and all things new. I call it the "Jewish centering prayer" because it helps me center on the miracle of the present moment, to focus on preciousness of any given point in time, and to be grateful for its holi-

does wonders."

29. David Steindl-Rast has written and taught much about radical gratefulness. See, for example, his book *Gratefulness, the Heart of Prayer*.

30. One of the traditional daily prayers that reminds me of what "right mindfulness" should entail says: "We thank you and recount your praise: for our lives, which are in your hands; for our souls, which are in your keeping; for your wondrous signs that are with us daily; and for your wonderful gifts and goodness at all times, evening, morning, and noon."

ness: "Praised are you, YHVH our God, Ruler of All, who has given us life, kept us alive, and enabled us to reach this moment."[31]

Ancient prayers such as this one still speak to me. In general though, as I try to cultivate an attitude of radical gratefulness, or when I offer a reflexive prayer, or when I meditate, I find that what the psalmist said long ago still works best for me: "To you, silence is praise."[32] And so, for now, I find that my silently thought feelings brought to conscious mind are my best, most heartfelt prayers, and I am grateful simply for existing and being alive to life's wonders and pains.

31. To my surprise, one evening when I met my good friend Ted Falcon for our monthly sushi and sake suppers, he began the evening with a toast using this blessing in exactly the same way as I do. He told me it's been his common practice for some time as well. He teaches that blessing opens us to the wonders of gratitude, and gratitude is the doorway to living in the present moment.

32. Teh/Ps 65:2.

Chapter 5

Acquiring Wisdom
Two Experiences

"But where can wisdom be found; / Where is the source of understanding?"
(IYOV 28:12)

THERE IS A GREAT difference between knowledge and wisdom. Knowledge derives from books and resides in the head; wisdom may include knowledge, but it is derived from life and resides in the heart or *kishkes*.[1] For many years, I had labored at obtaining knowledge and in this I was very successful. But when it comes to wisdom, I am a slow learner—or perhaps it is just a lifelong process. I do, however, recognize two experiences, one uplifting and one overwhelming, that were key transformational moments.

One year, as I was about to lead High Holy Day services, I looked out over the assembled people and saw several hundred individuals sitting before me. In the brief moment that it took, I suddenly grew aware of the fact that each of these people brought with them to this service a lifetime's worth of experiences. Here were all these beings, each with thoughts and feelings tucked away deep inside, yet simultaneously here were those same hidden things, floating like comic strip thought-bubbles above each person's head. I felt overwhelmed by the cacophony of all these lives, each

1. Literally "guts" or "intestines" in Yiddish.

with their private joys and secret sorrows, their silent fears and unspoken expectations.

At that moment, I was struck with a profound sense of compassion for everyone, myself included, for our physical and emotional limitations, for our ineptitude, for our valiant efforts and for our failings; and I thought, "Perhaps this is how God feels about us—like the parent of a toddler, who cannot but shake his head at the little one's attempts to cope with life."

I was struck with the thought the Abrahamic faiths envision a deity who alone can break through the barriers that separate us, one from the other; who can see into our souls, even into places where we ourselves are not honest enough or brave enough to look; who can relate to each of us, in our totality, yet who has energy to spare for all Creation; and that this conception of God is wonderful because this God so precisely transcends our most basic existential limitation: our sense of separateness. In that moment I wished that if this God did exist, he would come and heal us of all our secret wounds!

All this only took a few seconds and then the sensation passed. It was time to lead my congregation in prayer. And so we began—but I never felt the same towards a group of people again without having a moment of compassion for them all, myself included. This was the beginning of my acquiring wisdom: not to be too judgmental, and to have a little compassion (*rochmoness*, in Yiddish) for other people.

As sweet as this experience was, the second experience was its opposite—a spiritually and emotionally painful moment when the proverbial straw broke the camel's (i.e., my) back:

The evening that the doctor told me that my wife would have to undergo serious emergency surgery for her abdominal obstruction coincided with the first anniversary of my father's death. The latter event, called a *yahrzeit* in European Jewish tradition, is a significant annual occasion in Jewish mourning rituals. Emotional as it is, that *yahrzeit* was especially so because it was my father's first.

Since my father had died suddenly the year before, I had kept a picture of him on display for comfort.[2] That day, I left the hospital to come home, freshen up, light the memorial candle, and recite the traditional *kaddish* prayer. But as I gazed at his image, I was overwhelmed with sadness and

---

2. Sometimes I would look at his picture and just smile; other times I would shake my head at his picture and chide him for dying the way he did, without giving us a chance to say our farewells. (That may not have been logical, but it helped me cope with his sudden death.)

despair for all that had happened: the deaths of my brother-in-law and sister-in-law and my aunt and uncle, my wife's cancer, my mother's dangerous heart condition, my father's dropping dead, our daughter's recurring leukemia, and now my wife's emergency surgery.

As others before me have done, I sought to ease my pain not in prayer to God, but in alcohol. At first I took a drink to salute my dad's memory—which was ironic because he was almost a teetotaler. I wept as I recalled that I had not been able to bid him farewell because he had died so suddenly. Nor had I been able to mourn my father as I had wanted to, according to Jewish ways: I had had to leave the *shiva*, the seven-day initial mourning period, in Toronto, to fly back home to Seattle to be with my wife while she underwent chemotherapy in the hospital; I had been unable to attend the unveiling of my father's tombstone because our daughter was hospitalized with leukemia; and now I was unable to be in Toronto again for the first *yahrzeit* because my wife was about to undergo emergency abdominal surgery. And I was scared out of my mind about that! As I sat there lamenting and crying, I kept on drinking.

Grief had isolated me, even without my being aware of it. I had been seduced into being "the family strong one," and I felt I had no one to turn to. I couldn't bother my wife, who was in the hospital; I didn't want to upset our children more than they already were; I didn't want to disrupt our friends' holiday plans with my misery. I felt utterly alone.

Fortunately, even in her drugged-out state, my wife knew that something was amiss. She told several visiting friends that she thought I needed a shoulder to lean on, and they told several others, and before too long I was enveloped in lovingkindness. At first, I resisted. "I am strong," I said. "I am fine. My wife needs support, not me." But down deep I knew they were right, so I opened up and began to talk. Yes, I had been the strong one for my family, but even the strong have feelings, and I had been, and was still going through, quite an ordeal. So I talked, not just to friends and family, but also to a therapist. Gradually I regained my emotional and spiritual equilibrium, but it was an incredibly painful time.

So what does all this have to do with acquiring wisdom? Because of my work and my studies, I thought I was prepared to handle the experience of suffering. And initially I was. But emotional suffering and grief come not all at once; they are more like breaking waves, coming one after another, pounding on the breakwater of one's inner reserves, overwhelming them when one least expects it. Mishlei (Proverbs) says, "The ירא [awe/fear] of YHVH is the beginning of wisdom."[3] Curiously, in Hebrew the word for "awe" and "fear" is the same. Although I knew by now that God was not responsible for our travails, the number of crises we had endured brought me to the awe/fear of the random terror of disease and death in our lives. I was left feeling powerless.

From this low point in my life I learned two significant lessons and I hope that, unlike calculus, they stay with me the rest of my days. First, I learned to expect the unexpected, to let go of my plans and to live as fully as I can by seizing the moment. There is a Yiddish proverb that goes: "Man plans and God laughs." We all tend to spend life planning for the future, presuming that life is predictable. But it ain't—ever. We just like to delude ourselves by building up a façade of predictability over what is essentially random and chaotic. Although it is important to have dreams for the future and equally important to plan for them, one also has to remain somewhat unattached to them and let life run its uncharted course. I have learned again and again (and again) to try to live in the present, to grab joy and celebrate life in whatever possible way I could. Even in the direst of times, I could find joy, for example, in looking at my wife's face as she rested, or in our holding hands. There is an exquisite feeling, both wondrous and painful, that accompanies the awareness of life's preciously short duration. Would that I could maintain that feeling at all times.

Second, my sense of powerlessness in the face of suffering made me aware of my need of other people. Even though I often had preached about "building a community of compassion" during the eleven years I served as the director of Multifaith Works, I had never experienced it personally because I hadn't needed it. I learned that when one is in need a community of compassion of some sort will materialize to provide a personal safety net for that person. That support may come from family or friends, or it may not. It can also come from total strangers who are present simply because they care. But in order for it to happen, one has to take a risk; one has to risk being vulnerable; one has to ask for support. One just has to trust.

Some might have turned to God for support at such a point in their lives but it never occurred to me to try. Just as I didn't see God's hand in the suffering that I was experiencing, neither did I expect to find God's presence if I sought it out. For me, it was enough that I had the support of my fellow human beings—and perhaps that *is* where God's presence is found.

3. Mish/Prov 9:10.

Chapter 6

Elihu Intercedes I
In Which I'm Directed to Choose a Different Spiritual Path

"Truly, God does all these things / Two or three times to a man, / To bring him back from the pit, / That he may bask in the light of life."
(Iyov 33:29–30)

RABBIS INTERPRET THEIR COMMUNAL roles in a variety of ways. Many see themselves as custodians of Jewish tradition, or curators if you will, preserving and transmitting that tradition to all who are interested. For years I dismissed this function as necessary but less important than the role I had chosen for myself: a physician for the Jewish soul. It was—and it remains—my belief that the Jewish people has never gotten over the theological wound caused by the Holocaust; that the scar tissue that formed over the wound hides an imperfect healing because we have never really addressed the core problem.

As a "physician for the Jewish soul" I saw it as my responsibility to re-open that theological wound and get people talking about their theological questions and doubts. "Arguing with God" was my preferred medicine for what ailed us and whenever I would teach or lecture about "arguing with God," I would preach the same message over and over again:

It's kosher to be angry at God for what has happened to us and to use protest as a form of prayer. Look: here's a who's who of who has argued with God in the past: Avraham, Moshe, Yermiyahu (Jeremiah), Iyov . . . Levi Yitzhak . . . Elie Wiesel. Think about all we've suffered—Egyptians, Assyrians, Babylonians, Romans, Crusader massacres, European expulsions, Cossack massacres, Russian and Ukrainian pogroms, the Holocaust—come on, folks! Enough is enough! Let's all shout those words from Paddy Chayefsky's film *Network*: "We're mad as hell and we're not going to take it any more!" Now *that's* a modern Jewish prayer!

Then we'd all laugh rather nervously, relieved that I had not actually led them in such an angry prayer. No harm done. It was all just an intellectual exercise . . .

It was also a personal spiritual dead end. "Arguing with God" had been my spiritual practice for decades but I had taken it as far as I could. Without a biblical-type divine response, how long can one go on protesting? I knew I needed a new direction but I had a dilemma: I had built a mighty scholarly tower around me for protection but the problem with building a tower from the inside is that I had ended up being enclosed in a spiritual cell of my own making. It was becoming clear that I needed to break out—or be broken out.

I   THE AWE-FULLNESS OF GOD
STRIKES ME DOWN

With every class I taught, every service I led, every sermon I gave, I brought myself closer and closer to some ill-defined edge. Then, one Rosh Hashanah, I skirted a little too close to that edge, leaned over and confronted that which is nameless, awe-full, and fearsome. I was struck down in a heap. (Or so it appeared to me.)

One of the Torah portions read on Rosh Hashanah is the story of the binding, or near-sacrifice, of Yitzhak (Isaac), by his father Avraham, at God's command, and of God's last-minute intervention to prevent that sacrifice from occurring. Traditionally, the story is viewed as a test of Avraham's faithfulness and his complete trust in God and/or as a test of Yitzhak's willingness to be a sacrifice, a martyr. That particular year, I wanted to preach on whether we can know what God really wants of us. I wanted people specifically to ask themselves how Avraham knew that what he heard as

God's command to sacrifice his son actually was God's command and not some dark deviancy of his own devising. To dramatize this idea, I planned to read God's words in the Torah portion in a stage whisper rather than chanted aloud as is customary.

I was in fine form that day, confident and self-assured. But by the third line of the Torah reading I knew I was in trouble. Perhaps it was the fact that I hadn't eaten that morning; perhaps it was due to my lack of voice training that made me hyperventilate as I stage-whispered God's words; perhaps I was ambushed by the dramatic emotional effect the recitation had on me—to this day I do not know for sure—but I choked on the words, grew hot and then light-headed, and finally broke away from the lectern to collapse in a faint.

Pandemonium broke out in the congregation. Now, had this been an evangelical Christian church, everyone might have been on their feet shouting "Praise Jesus!" at this outbreak of the Holy Spirit, but since this was a Reform Jewish congregation, people cried out "*Oy gevalt*! Is there a doctor in the house?" Surprisingly, there was only one. I came to with a hundred faces anxiously peering down at me. I took something to drink and a candy, finished services, and later let my wife take me for a check-up. The doctor said I had a tendency towards hypoglycemia and told me that I had to eat regularly.

That explained everything . . .

But it didn't really, because I alone knew what I had been feeling as I had grown dizzy. As I whispered God's words, I thought of my own little daughter—or was it me as a son?—and what it *really* would feel like to be commanded to kill one's own child and then actually to seek to do it. I felt a dread overcome me, my blood congealed in my belly, I shrank back in horror, attempted to flee—and fainted dead away. For the next ten days I was literally without energy, a nervous wreck. I managed to lead Yom Kippur services only by holding on, white-knuckled, to the lectern.

When I look back on this awe-full event, I realize that all explanations as to why I fainted are valid and probable. My doctor and my therapist and my friend the actor all had their own rationales, but I have mine. I choose to remember the event primarily as a spiritual experience, and not a very pleasant one at that. I had been touched by the dread of the divine and reminded of the limits of my power. I was jolted in the midst of my spiritual journey and "encouraged" to move on.

II A VOICE FROM THE DEAD CHANGES MY LIFE DIRECTION

In the 1980s and early 90s, I was working as community relations director for the Jewish Federation of Greater Seattle. My job was to bring together all the diverse organizations and congregations in the Jewish community—Orthodox, Conservative, Reform, humanists, Democrats and Republicans, hawkish Zionists and dovish Zionists, and more besides—and to work with all of them to seek consensus positions on issues both domestic and international. Practically speaking, this was a thankless task because it meant that I either was being criticized by the community's left wing for being too conservative or attacked by the right wing for being too liberal. After ten years of this stereo *kvetching*, I knew I needed to move on to a new position. But until I found it I was locked in my career, just as I found myself spiritually blocked by arguing with God as well. That's when a voice from the dead gave me the encouragement to forge a new trail for my life . . .

I was riding in my car, returning home from having taught yet one more class on the Jewish tradition of arguing with God. My new cassette of Bob Marley and the Wailers was on the tape deck. I was listening intently, enjoying the music and the message. And then I heard it: Bob Marley chanting from beyond the grave, "One love, one heart, let's get together and feel all right . . . If Anson prays to the Lord, then it will be all right."

I nearly drove off the road! Talk about reefer madness—could he really be addressing me? What was he telling me about my stubborn refusal to pray to the God for whom I only had anger? I was shaking as I rewound the tape and played it again. Ah, there was the problem—it was his Jamaican accent: "One love, one heart, let's get together and feel all right . . . (G)ive (d)ance-an(d) praise to the Lord, then I will be all right." "Give dance and praise"—not "if Anson prays." I chuckled with relief and laughed at my own foolishness.

But as I listened to the song again and again—and, though I knew Bob Marley wasn't addressing me specifically (thank God)—I realized that he was talking to me, soothing me, telling me it was time, time to let go of some of my anger, to open my soul to love, my heart to joy, and my being to compassion. Perhaps, by doing these things, there would even come a day when I would let myself actually be able to pray again. He told me: "Don't worry about a thing, 'cause every little thing gonna be all right . . . this is my message to you."

Soon after, I took a new job for the better when I was hired as the executive director of the Multifaith Works, a non-profit organization that provided supportive housing and spiritual care to people living with and dying from AIDS. It was 1993 and AIDS was a major crisis in America, then still an epidemic that provoked fear and loathing in many people's minds.

Despite my misgivings about doing pastoral work, helping people who really needed support and doing so on an interfaith basis greatly appealed to me. I began working with people who faced disease and death on a daily basis. It was a plunge into the deep end of human suffering and it changed my life completely.

I commenced an apprenticeship in the practice of lovingkindness under the tutelage of some of the most wonderful people I have ever known. Whether coworker or client or volunteer, all conspired, as it were, to help me climb out of the spiritual hole I had dug for myself by focusing solely and for too long on arguing with God.

Working with people with AIDS forced me to confront the issue of personal suffering head on. I observed that many individuals dealing with a terminal illness react to suffering no differently than does the collective consciousness of an entire people. Both wrestle with the issue of God's presence in the face of suffering: "Where is God when suffering happens?" "Does God know what is happening?" "Is God responsible for my suffering?" "Did I do something to deserve this?" "Who or what is God?"

As we struggled together through grief, remorse, anger, and bewilderment, I began to look at God in new ways, to view pastoral counseling and prayer with new respect, to see how much our various faith traditions have in common, and to regard hands-on service as one of the best ways one can live one's faith. It is an adage in the AIDS community that in helping others a person in fact gets more than s/he gives, and I have found this to be so for me as well. I learned so much about life, about other people, and about myself. I know I became a more compassionate and less judgmental human being as a result.

Chapter 7

Elihu Intercedes II
How a Chinese-Jewish Theology Helped My Spiritual Growth

"Be still, and I will teach you wisdom."
(Iyov 33:33)

I   ABOUT THE CHINESE JEWS OF KAIFENG

WE OFTEN HAVE NO idea of the extent to which Judaism has borrowed from other theologies and philosophies down through the ages. The foundations of biblical Judaism are found in ancient Egyptian, Mesopotamian, and Canaanite cultures. Post-exilic, proto-rabbinic Judaism borrowed from the Zoroastrian faith and Hellenistic thought. Medieval rabbinic Judaism nourished itself on Aristotelian thought via Islamic thinkers and from Islam itself. In Europe, Jewish thinkers adopted and adapted ideas from Christian theologians and philosophers through the centuries down to our own day. We are doing it now in America too. This is what Jews everywhere have always done in order to survive and grow. Similarly, although tiny in numbers, the Chinese Jews of Kaifeng blazed a trail that was unique for its cultural adaptation and spiritual synthesis.

I "discovered" the Kaifeng Jews by accident while wandering the East Asian Library stacks at York University and coming upon a hefty volume in the entitled *Chinese Jews* by Bishop William Charles White, who had headed the Anglican mission in Kaifeng back at the beginning of the twentieth century. When I studied in China in 1973–74, I tried unsuccessfully to travel to Kaifeng but it was still closed to foreigners on account of the Cultural Revolution. Two years later found me in Cincinnati, Ohio on the campus of the Hebrew Union College (HUC) beginning my second year of rabbinical school. (The first year is spent in Israel doing intensive Hebrew language study.) At HUC Cincinnati, I found out that its Klau Library is one of the main repositories of manuscripts from the Kaifeng Jews and the librarians allowed me to see their collection in the rare books room. Knowing of my interest in the subject, when Michael Pollak contacted them regarding research he was doing for his celebrated book *Mandarins, Jews and Missionaries*, they put me in touch with him. A decade later, Pollak was kind enough to include me in the gathering of scholars and activists in Palo Alto that led to the founding of the Sino-Judaic Institute. I became the editor of its journal, *Points East*, and eventually its president for a time.

One day I received a letter addressed to me as the editor of *Points East* from nearby Victoria, British Columbia. It was from a former professor of mine at York University, a Jewish sinologist named Jordan Paper,[1] who had tried (with meager results) to teach me classical Chinese. He had retired and relocated to Victoria with his wife and now was reaching out to me in my capacity as editor of *Points East*. We became colleagues and then friends. Several years later, he asked me to write a postscript to his book *The Theology of the Chinese Jews* in which I attempted to apply the theology of Chinese Jews to the contemporary post-Holocaust Jewish experience, and in 2017 he and I edited a collection of scholarly essays on the Kaifeng Jews past and present.[2]

As I struggled professionally and personally with Jewish spirituality—and as I was simultaneously learning more about the Kaifeng Jews—I began to think that perhaps the Kaifeng Jewish materials, recorded for posterity by Jesuit and other missionaries, might have something of value to offer the spiritually restless souls of our post-Holocaust, contemporary world. What I didn't realize at the time was that it would be spiritually worthwhile for me personally as well.

---

1. Professor Emeritus of East Asian and Religious Studies at York University.
2. Laytner and Paper, *Chinese Jews of Kaifeng*.

Because they lived in China, the Kaifeng Jews borrowed from Daoist and Confucian thought as they settled into their new cultural home.[3] The incorporation of Chinese ideas into Kaifeng Jewish religious thought represents a unique synthesis. Admittedly, this Sino-Judaism has not had any influence in the history of Jewish thought as did, for example, the incorporation of Hellenistic thought into proto-rabbinic Judaism, which evolved into the Judaism that is practiced today, and which also laid some of the foundations for Christianity and Islam, but it is nonetheless significant in its own right.

The Kaifeng Jews wanted to have their faith and practices be understood in light of the dominant culture, much as Jews everywhere always have. In the Chinese situation, they were fortunate to live in a society that fostered syncretism and was indifferent to doctrinal differences in a way unimaginable in the monotheistic Middle East, North Africa, or Europe. Consequently, the Kaifeng community was able to embrace basic Confucian and Daoist concepts and relatively easily blend them with their own Jewish ones. The focus of both Confucianism and Judaism on human relationships rather than theology made this synthesis particularly rich and it was able to sustain the community for many centuries.[4]

II   A KAIFENG JEWISH THEOLOGY

When talking about God, the Kaifeng texts use the term *Tian*, which is not a proper name or even a word meaning "God," like the Hebrew *El* or *Elohim*. Like its Hebrew counterpart, *Shamayim*, *Tian* is a word with a dual meaning, referring both to the actual sky and to a figurative or symbolic "Heaven." It is impersonal, even abstract. Rather than using the anthropomorphisms of the Torah, Talmud, and prayer book—terms like father, king

3. Jordan Paper in *The Theology of the Chinese Jews* has drawn attention to the cultural bias of the dominant Ashkenazi Jewish community when it comes to examining the so-called exotic Jewish communities, which renders their Jewish culture "inauthentic." Its attitude towards the Kaifeng community is part and parcel of this bias. Thus, while it may indeed be said that the Chinese Jews absorbed foreign ideas into their faith, the same may be said, and indeed ought to be said, about the Jewish communities of Europe and the Middle East as well. What is fit for the Beijing duck ought to be fit for the goose and gander as well!

4. That the Kaifeng community almost ceased to exist is due to its small numbers and long isolation, to the integration of its members into the larger society, and to China's own long eclipse during the late Qing dynasty and the subsequent turmoil of the early republic.

and so on—the Chinese Jewish texts assert that the divine, i.e., Heaven, is a mystery, as something truly beyond our comprehension. This is hardly an alien idea for it is precisely what both the Jewish philosopher Maimonides and the Jewish mystics taught as well.

Closely related to "Heaven" is their use of the word *Dao*, or "Way," which is both another name for God and also their term of choice for Torah. As the former, both God and *Dao* are singular; they precede all that exists and also encompass everything that exists.[5] With regards the latter, their choice was a good one because the concepts of Torah and *Dao* can fit neatly together. For the rabbis, Torah—which literally means instruction, and in this case divine instruction—existed in multiple forms: Written, Oral, and primordial. According to classical rabbinic midrashim, the primordial Torah existed before Creation and God used it, as an architect might use a blueprint, to effect Creation.[6] In this form, Torah suggests something greater than "Torah" as we generally understand the word but, at the same time, it is markedly similar to the concept of the *Dao*—although the latter lacks the divine activism and anthropomorphisms. The key point, however, is that both Torah and *Dao* are accessible to human beings because, through meditation, prayer, and study, a person can gain both an understanding of Creation/the *Dao* and knowledge of how to live one's life in harmony with this heavenly order.

One of the bigger differences between the Chinese Jewish "theology" and mainstream Jewish theology has to do with the concepts of revelation and God's intervention in history. In the Chinese Jewish texts, Heaven's only intervention—if it is that at all—is the giving of Scriptures. *Tian*, Heaven, can be perceived both through the creative power of nature and through the Torah, both of which are called the *Dao* (or Way) of Heaven. Revelation is the attunement of the human being with the *Dao*, which is omnipresent and immanent. It is the role of the exceptional human being to perceive it, experience it, and try to communicate it to other people.

In the Chinese Jewish view, it is through human endeavor and self-improvement—not unlike Maimonides's views on the levels of the intellect and the prophetic mind—that an outstanding person like Avraham or Moshe can gain enlightenment and perceive the *Dao* of Heaven. In

5. For more on this topic, see Paper, *Theology of the Chinese Jews*, 110–13. See also essays by Andrew Plaks and Irene Eber in Laytner and Paper, *Chinese Jews of Kaifeng*.

6. *Genesis Rabbah* 1:1. Sometimes the opening sentence of *Genesis* was translated/interpreted as "With Wisdom [i.e., Torah], God created heaven and earth."

Avraham's case, his enlightened state made him the first to "know" Heaven and therefore he is honored as the founder of the faith. In Moshe's case, his highly developed personal character led to his perceiving the mystery of Heaven and then to his composing the Scriptures and the commandments therein. But the revelation was theirs to achieve, not God's to bestow. Absent from the texts is any substantive reference to Yisrael's miraculous Exodus from Egypt or its biblical years, the Covenant, and to God's use of history and nature as either reward or punishment.

Lastly, what emerges as most striking about the Kaifeng Jewish materials is their humanistic focus. The ordinary person has only to practice the *Dao* as expressed in the Torah, i.e., the *mitzvot*, or commandments—honoring Heaven with appropriate prayers and rituals, respecting one's ancestors, and living ethically—in order to put oneself in harmony simultaneously with the *Dao* of the natural world and the *Dao* of Heaven. For the Chinese Jews, as for Jews everywhere, the *mitzvot*, the commandments, also provided for Jewish continuity. They constitute "Jewish civilization" and wherever Jews wandered, there too went the *mitzvot*. The Kaifeng Jews were traditionalists in their observance but they embellished their practice with Chinese aesthetics and values. Their adoption and adaptation of the Chinese *rujia* tradition (mistakenly called Confucianism by some people) stressed the importance of personal spiritual development, the need for self-evaluation/self-cultivation, and individual responsibility vis-à-vis the community as integral parts of observing the *mitzvot*. This is comparable to the traditional Jewish practices of *heshbon hanefesh* (taking account of one's deeds) and *teshuvah* (repentance, i.e., returning to path of Torah). One engaged in self-cultivation not just for one's own sake, but because one's personal ethical behavior shows respect for one's ancestors, demonstrates responsibility to the community in the present, and provides a model for future generations to emulate.

This sense of connection with the past and future was probably heightened for the Kaifeng Jews by their adoption of Chinese cultural norms of *xiao* (filial piety) and "ancestor reverence." Ancestor reverence gave them a unique sense of being contemporary links in the chain of a proud and ancient civilization. It was a way of honoring and connecting with the past and emphasizing the responsibility of the present generation to prepare the way for the future. Although much more intense than normative Jewish practice, *xiao* has its counterparts in commandments such as honoring one's parents and respecting elders, and in mourning customs such as observing the anniversaries of one's parents' deaths.

What I appreciated from my study of the Kaifeng Jews' theology was their emphasis on human behavior combined with ritual practice, and on the ability of individuals to perceive an immanent Presence in the world. Their thinking provided me with an alternative to a system based on a supernatural God's intervening in history and waiting for God to intervene in history once again. Theirs was a faith firmly planted on earth and grounded in the proper doing of daily deeds. Their practice was meant to enable them to feel a sense of unity with past and future generations, with the totality of the natural world and with Heaven itself.

What came to matter most to me from my study of this community's theology was its emphasis on inwardness. It was what I wanted for myself. While I knew a little about the contemplative tradition in Jewish mysticism and Hasidism, it didn't resonate with me the way the Kaifeng Judeo-Daoist approach did. Probably it had to do with the complex theologizing of the former as opposed to the simplicity of the latter, which stressed attunement and mystery. From the Kaifeng Jews I felt a historical validation that meditation and seeking union with the divine were legitimate Jewish activities. Their teachings came to inform my desire to seek balance and harmony and inner peace in life, to accept both good and evil as part of life, and to aspire for a connection between my mind/heart/soul/*neshama*/*chi* and God/*Tian*/YHVH/the *Dao*.

Chapter 8

Iyov's Theophany I
Letting Go of God to Find God

"I had heard of you with my ears, / But now I see you with my eyes."
(Iyov 42:5)

I   A DIVINE EXPERIENCE

JUST AS IN THE book of Iyov, what Iyov's "friends" believe they know about God—what we claim to know about God—is what our holy books and faith traditions say God has revealed about *himself* and *his* plan. Then we cite these texts as proof of what we know—a rather circular arrangement, convincing only to ourselves. Initially, Iyov thought similarly to his friends, until he instigated his lawsuit and forced God to appear. His experience of God transformed his perspective. So too with me:

I was just a young man, in my late adolescence, still living in my parents' home, when I had my first taste of what I called "the divine." It was a summer's day, in the afternoon, and I was hiking in the ravine that lay below our home. Birds were singing, insects were flying about, the sun was shining, and a gentle breeze made the tree leaves shimmer with light. It was, in all respects, a normal summer's day. But as I walked along I suddenly became aware of everything altogether: the birds, the insects, the trees, the stream, the earth, the air, and me. We were one; or rather, everything I normally experienced as being outside myself, together with a sense of experiencing myself outside of myself—a sort of out of body sensation—were part of some whole Oneness. Initially, I felt myself lose significance and blend into my surroundings. Then I seemed to shrink in size as my perspective drew me further and further away from where I stood on the earth's surface. Finally, even as I felt my self merging deliciously into this Whole, I felt the sun's rays falling upon my head and shoulders, and just as suddenly as I had felt this sweet sensation of oneness—and yet without losing any of this sensation—I now felt a profound sense of my own uniqueness. The sun's rays were kissing me, only me, the only me that ever was or will be. I was at once part of and at one with all Creation, yet simultaneously a unique and distinct being. I felt love and peace and joy. I was totally, wholly tranquil. And then the sensation passed. I walked on in a "holy" daze.

What I had experienced was unlike anything I had ever learned about God in Jewish school or in formal prayer. Spirituality and the mystical experience were not exactly the coin in trade of the Canadian Reform Jewish congregation in which I grew up and was educated, nor was it part of my family's religious vocabulary. Nonetheless, I called my experience "becoming aware of God." Why did I call it "God"? I called it "God" because, as a Jew, it felt right to do so—although I certainly wasn't associating my experience with all that God had come to mean. From my encounter, I just knew that God—"Something Greater"—is present in our world and that this Presence is good—how else could I interpret being bathed in the paradoxical but intensely beautiful sense of unity and uniqueness I had felt?

Years later, I learned a Hasidic saying that taught that a person should go through life as if wearing a coat with two pockets.[1] Each pocket contains a message. In one pocket are written the words "For my sake the world was created," and in the other pocket the words "I am but dust and ashes." One's life, therefore, ought to be a balancing act between these two standards of self-perception. I was that coat with pockets of finite individuality and infinite unity!

My taste of the divine was the beginning of a lifelong spiritual journey.

II   NAKED SPIRITUALITY

In the Abrahamic traditions, when we consider God, we usually start from the heavens and look down, that is, we commence with a divine revelation.

1. By the Hasidic rebbe Simcha Bunim of Peshischa, Poland (1765–1827).

Instead, we should start with ourselves and pursue the subject of knowing God from the ground up. My Episcopal priest friend, Mary Jane Francis, told me that Anglican Christianity in fact tries to do theology "from below," meaning that it starts with experience and builds from there.

So, let's start with ourselves. Imagine a naked person. In terms of physical characteristics, we all look basically the same—we are, after all, one species, just in various shades of beige. Now put clothes on that naked body. The wearing of clothes is something we all do yet at the same time we also use clothes to distinguish us, one from the other, in terms of culture, class, generation, and gender.

Now imagine that naked person again. In terms of general spiritual characteristics, we also are basically the same. Every person, by virtue of being a human being, shares certain spiritual characteristics, just as we do physical ones. This should hardly be surprising. These spiritual characteristics include a variety of needs and concerns: the desire to have meaning in one's life, to know love and feel companionship, to have a set of morals and values, to live a life of hope, and to sense some connection with something that transcends the individual self.

I find it hard to imagine that are any people without spiritual issues when confronting suffering and death. When we confront our mortality, we might find ourselves facing spiritual needs and issues that had been long and deeply suppressed, such as: completing unfinished business in one's relationships; concerns about love, reconciliation and forgiveness; anxiety about one's deeds and misdeeds; and, of course, questions about God. Then, suddenly, these issues and needs acquire an urgency they never had previously. To face these crises without any spiritual clothing can be cold indeed!

Most people use a faith community (whether inherited or chosen) to cover their naked spirituality. Our various religions are the spiritual clothes we wear, yet at the same time we also use them to distinguish us, one from the other. Just as material clothing comes in a variety of styles, so too do religions offer various designs for belief, life cycle rituals, forms of worship, and types of community. And, over time, each faith grows more and more specific about what clothes (i.e., the beliefs and rituals) its adherents may or may not wear.

At one point or another in their lives, many people will look at the spiritual clothes they are wearing and ask themselves if they really are a good fit. Perhaps they've gotten a little too constrictive; maybe they are too juvenile in appearance, or just plain out of date. As people examine their spiritual outfits, they cannot help but focus on the central feature of each outfit: God. How humanity has styled God down through the ages has resulted in a variety of conflicting high-end concepts. God is singular or plural; visible or invisible; transcendent or immanent or both; male, female, both and neither; eternal, resurrecting, or reincarnating; etc., etc. Religions are hard pressed to confine perceptions of God to just a few authorized fashion statements.

In my case, I grew up comfortably wearing Jewish spiritual clothes. Later, after my experience of the divine, I began to wonder how my spiritual experience connected with the God of my inherited tradition. As I explored the connection between the two, I found another Hasidic teaching that touched me profoundly. Yisrael ben Eliezer, the Baal Shem Tov, the eighteenth-century East European Jewish mystic who founded the Hasidic movement, taught that there are two reasons why many of the Jewish liturgy's basic prayers begin with the words "Our God and God of our ancestors." The first: that there are two ways of knowing God—through personal experience (our God) and through inherited tradition (God of our ancestors). The second: that the two phrases are linked together as one so that we know that our personal and individual experiences of God are integrally connected to that which our ancestors also experienced.

To me this meant that we not only have the recorded experiences of previous generations to draw upon reverentially—but not to be idolized—we have our own experiences of God as well, and these should not be dismissed. The phrase "Our God and God of our ancestors" is both a blessing and a curse, because what we experience anew is limited and constrained—and also expanded and broadened—by the spiritual heritages of our various faith traditions. Being part of a faith tradition—or any kind of community—means that one links one's own experiences up with one's collective past. We are like coral, the living edge of a great reef reaching up to the light, standing upon the ideas of generations of dead ancestors and building upon their foundations with our own experiences of God. Both perceptions are necessary for individual and collective spiritual survival.

At the same time I gradually became aware that, because of my spiritual experience, some of my inherited spiritual clothes no longer fit quite right. My "arguing with God" outfit was the last spiritual outfit that featured a traditional Jewish conception of God. The more I probed conventional rationalizations for suffering and other beliefs about this traditional God, the more I realized I had to try on a spiritual outfit that was designed around a different God-concept. I needed a different way to think about God.

III GOD IS GREATER

At one stage in my life, I focused my time on pondering the meaning of the Covenant and the special relationship Jewish tradition says Jews have with God. Today the issue of being God's "chosen people" seems too parochial; it seems absurd to think this way any longer. Can God really be so concerned with the affairs of one small people? Yes, the Jewishly perceived God can be, and the Christianly perceived God is equally concerned about the church. Indeed, I wonder if there is a nation or a faith anywhere that has not considered itself "God's chosen" or "beloved," the figurative center of the world or most important country/tribe/faith of all. Individually and collectively, we never seem to completely lose our childlike desire to be the center of the universe, the apple of God's eye.

Today, however, the world is smaller than it once was; we know more than ever before about one another thanks to advances in travel and communication. We now know that many faiths and peoples have considered themselves God's favorite. Even in the best expressions of traditional religion, the universal God of the Jews is still attached to the Jews and the land of Israel; the universal God of Christianity is bonded to the church; the universal God of Islam reveals his word only in Arabic—and even Zen Buddhist ceremonies, rituals, and meditation are best performed in Japanese style!

Our efforts at describing God are like the story of the blind men and the elephant: Six blind men were asked to determine what an elephant looked like by feeling different parts of the elephant's body. One blind man felt a leg and said the elephant was like a pillar; the one who felt the tail said the elephant was like a rope; the one who felt the trunk said the elephant was thick as a tree limb; the one who felt the ear said the elephant was broad and flat like a hand fan; the one who felt the side said the elephant was like a wall; and the one who felt the tusk said the elephant was like a pipe.

Was any one of them wrong? No. But was any one of them completely right? No again. Because they couldn't see, they couldn't see what an entire elephant looks like and so identified the whole by the part they had felt. In fact, however, an elephant has all the features they experienced and more.

I use this famous story to describe our relationship with the divine. What we call "God" is ultimately an indescribable mystery to limited creatures such as ourselves. But then we then turn around and insist on defining the divine by our limited experiences, just like the blind men in the parable. However, God is beyond all these borders of our own perceptions. Rather, God belongs to us all, however and whatever we perceive God to be, no matter how we choose to dress and address the divine.

I like to liken the divine to an infinitely faceted gemstone, one that simultaneously offers many different perspectives for observation.[2] Each individual, each generation, and every faith over time is capable of describing only a few divine facets—but no one individual and no one faith can ever know the whole gemstone—that remains beyond our human capabilities. Put all the facets together and you get a much better—but still incomplete—picture of how humanity imagines the divine mystery.

The divine imaginings that result from our individual and collective spiritual experiences point to a shared truth: *Humanity generally yearns to connect with something that is somehow greater than all of us, something transcendent.* For the Abrahamic faiths this transcendence is called "God," while for others, Buddhism and Hinduism for example, it is the ultimate reality behind this world of illusion and attachment. One might even claim that a secular political system like communism or fascism—or devotion to a nation-state—demonstrates a yearning for connection with something transcendent. Regardless of how the transcendent is viewed, every religion has designed distinctive spiritual outfits—systems of belief, ritual, and practice—based upon their unique perspectives. Each has its own unique validity. But our theologies and our religions are our metaphysical constructs, not eternal verities. To speak in monotheistic terms, they represent conceptions based upon perceptions of God; they do not represent God the ineffable, who exceeds all our imaginings, past, present, and future. The sum of God-concepts is greater than all its parts and the total will always amount to mystery.

What is called for is a little spiritual humility on our part. If we have spiritual humility, then we will acknowledge that God is greater than anything we can say about God and that all our faiths are flawed because they

---

2. James Eblen, my friend and colleague, and professor emeritus at Seattle University School of Theology and Ministry, told me that in Native American prayer circles a rock is placed in its center to represent the divine.

are all based on our incapability and incapacity to perceive the wholeness that is God.

Spiritual humility means not confusing a system of beliefs with the mystery that is God; it means realizing that whatever one believes is only a human construct. Beliefs are our spiritual assumptions imposed on reality; faith is accepting these beliefs as being real. The fact that I don't believe the same thing as you doesn't make it wrong; it's just different. And the fact that we may disagree does not make my beliefs any less important or valuable to me, or to my faith community, or to humanity.

Religious traditions that are based on the mystic experience offer an alternative to beliefs about God. The mystic experience is not unintelligible, particularly to those who have had a similar experience, and these spiritual testimonies are increasingly being recorded and studied.[3] The mystic experience, which I now call what I had as a young man, shares common features regardless of cultural context, and thus exposes the human spirituality that stands naked under the clothes of our various religious traditions. It breaks through doctrinal ideas about God to reveal the ineffable mystery at the heart of so many of our faiths.

Accepting our limited human ability to know God means that we ought to respect our differences and our variations for the limited human creations they are; it means setting aside centuries of religious and ethnic intolerance; it means seeking to practice the ideals of our respective faiths and allowing others to do the same; it means finally learning to live and work together; and it means talking and listening as we share our experiences and understandings of the divine, always remembering that, whatever we think or say, God is greater.

IV A PLEA TO LET GOD BE

In Hebrew, the word for "God" is *Elohim* or *El* or *Elo'ah*, all cognately related to the Arabic *Allah*. But what does "God"—*Elohim*—mean? Strictly speaking, *Elohim* is not a name; it's a job title, and one that many ancient Near Eastern deities were given by their peoples.[4] But for Jews God also has a personal name, several of them in fact . . .

3. See Paper, *Mystic Experience*, 11–51.

4. Thus Yaakov vows after his vision of the ladder that if YHVH will do "x" and "y" for him, then YHVH will be his *elohim* (god); the implication being that if YHVH fails to help him, then Yaakov is free to choose another, higher performing deity. See Ber/

95

In Shemot (Exodus) 3, in what is almost a humorous skit,[5] after encountering God in a talking burning bush, Moshe asks for God's name. Imagine Moshe's consternation when God replies, *Ehyeh-Asher-Ehyeh*, meaning "I am/will be who/what I am/will be." God tells Moshe to use that name when he speaks in God's name to Paro (Pharaoh) and the Israelites. God also says to Moshe, "You may also call me *Ehyeh* ['I will be'] for short." What a sense of humor! Imagine going up against the king of the greatest empire of its day and demanding: "Thus says '*I will be*,' Let my people go." No wonder Moshe had trouble convincing Paro to do his bidding!

God has another, related name, comprised of the Hebrew letters *yud*, *hay*, *vav*, and *hay*, which may be rendered in English letters as YHVH, and it is used throughout the Bible and in Jewish prayers to this day. Scholars call this name the Tetragrammaton, which is Greek for "four letters." In Jewish tradition YHVH is unutterable, both because it is believed to be God's holy, ineffable name and also because its pronunciation, which only the high priest knew, was lost when the Temple was destroyed. Biblical scholars often pronounce it as "Yahweh"—but who knows? (Personally, I believe YHVH to be the sound of breath entering and leaving our bodies and should be "pronounced" accordingly—"Yah," breathe in; "Veh," breathe out.)[6]

When Jews see the letters YHVH, we say "*Adonai*," meaning "Lord," and most Bible translations and Jewish prayer books follow this convention.[7] Traditional Jews call YHVH "*HaShem*," which simply means "The Name." That Name, YHVH, has a special meaning that says a great deal about the Jewish perception of God. The letters YHVH represent a combination of the present and future tenses of the verb meaning "to be." So God's name is literally (and grammatically) pure potential: Is-ness, Will Be-ing, Shall Be.[8] But what does this mean?

Gen 28:20–22.

5. In fact, Joseph Heller, in *God Knows*, 33–35, made it a humorous skit.

6. See Michaelson, *Everything Is God*, 47–49, for references to how other contemporary scholar/theologians discuss YHVH.

7. In Jewish tradition, it is entirely proper to use a diminutive for God's personal name, like using Rob in place of Robert, or Sue rather than Susan. Instead of *Ehyeh* or YHVH, we can say "*Yah*" as in "*Hallelu Yah*." Another name: Christians later took the vowels of *Adonai*, placed them under the Tetragrammaton, and, since the Y and J were interchangeable sounds, switched the Y for a J, and the world got "Jehovah." Thus God acquired yet another name.

8. The latter pseudonym is suggested by Michael Fishbane in his profound book

The name YHVH suggests that God's essence is forward looking and future oriented, as in fact the Torah has God say by way of self-description. After the golden calf fiasco, Moshe again asks to know God. But God says: "You cannot see my face, only my back,"[9] meaning, "You can only see where I've been, but that is not me, for I am in movement, always in the present/ future." So Moshe is only allowed to view God's passing by, much as we might see the wake of a ship without actually seeing the ship itself pass in front of us. It means that the Jewishly perceived God is always in a state of becoming. In other words, God is not yet whatever God will be; God is not perfect but may be said to be in a state of ongoing perfectibility.[10]

Traditionally, Judaism, like many other faiths, has accepted the premise that God is essentially unknowable.[11] Among classic medieval Jewish theologies, Rambam's (Maimonides) *via negativa*—using negative attributes to describe God—stands out as the most respectful way of expressing all we don't know about God. However, as in the cases of many other religions, rabbis down through the ages spent much effort trying to define YHVH philosophically and to enshrine only certain perceptions of YHVH as legitimate—Maimonides included.[12] But that effort, well intentioned though it was, has resulted over time in ossified perceptions of God, particularly in the popular mind. Once any single perception of God is given the mantle of absolute truth, it becomes a humanly sanctified image—an idol, so to speak—for subsequent generations. As opposed to this, thinking of God as YHVH is the essence of the second of the Ten Utterances (Commandments): not to make any images of the divine.[13] It keeps one's sense of God fresh—and a fresh God is a living God.

Sacred Attunement.

9. Shem/Exod 33:18–23.

10. For more on this interpretation, see Green, *Radical Judaism, and Ehyeh*. It also connects nicely with the God-concept of process theology, about which, from a Jewish perspective, see Artson, *God of Becoming and Relationship*, and Lubarsky and Griffin, *Jewish Theology and Process Thought*.

11. Nonetheless, supremely pragmatic *for a religion*, Judaism basically says: "We can't really know anything concrete about YHVH, but we *do* know the way we are supposed to act because God gave us the commandments." See Dev/Deut 29:28 and 30:11–14, for example.

12. See, for example, Lesley Hazelton's short take on this subject in her book *Agnostic*, 25–52.

13. To see how this concept of YHVH was developed in later medieval Judaism, see the first three of the Thirteen Principles of Maimonides (1135–1204) and the opening lines of Daniel ben Yehudah's *Yigdal* poem-prayer (circa 1300).

The name YHVH means that God is always beyond our limited abilities of comprehension; that God cannot be contained or controlled, summoned like a genie from a bottle, or confined by our desire to define. We may think we know God in some way through past deeds attributed to God, or through our own experiences, but that should never constrain what God is, because God is ultimately a mystery and will be whatever God will be. And this is precisely what God reserves for God's self in the theophany in the book of Iyov by declaring that he and his deeds are beyond our limited understanding.

Because I trust my experience, I know God exists. (I also know I was not delusional.) Nonetheless, despite what I perceive as my encounter with the divine, God remains a mystery to me. I think that is how it should be. Even in our closest human relationships, there are some barriers we can never transcend, such as fully comprehending all the experiences that contribute to the formation of another person's character. And if that is how it is between human beings in our most intimate relationships, how much the more so when it comes to our ability to "know" God?

To exist is to change and to experience change. Dare we permit ourselves to say the same about God? Can God remain the same when we have not, either as peoples in history or as individuals?[14] Just as we are usually defined or known by our past deeds, so too we tend to define God by his reported past deeds. But YHVH cannot be confined by the past. YHVH is present and future, so we need to let go of old theological concepts—even cherished, hallowed, time-honored concepts of God—in order to let God be YHVH. We need the freedom to perceive God in our own ways; to re-invent God, as it were, for our own day and our own needs. What we are changing is not God, only our God-concepts. We are only admitting our collective, limited ability to "know God." Dare we assert "There is a God" while admitting that we haven't a clue about who/what God is or what God

14. How unlike this view of God is from later understandings of God in all of the Abrahamic traditions, which view God as perfect, unchanging, and omni-everything. Reading the Tanakh (Bible), we see no indication that God is perfect and unchanging. Instead, the Bible depicts God changing his mind, regretting some of his deeds, getting angry, and sometimes doing things that are downright disturbing, even scary. That is far from being perfect. But perceptions of God changed—just look at how much better-behaved God appears to be by the rabbinic era. But do not take my word for it, look at how God also is depicted in the Christian Bible or in the Qur'an too. The God the Abrahamic faiths share, conceived in the early centuries of the Common Era, is a far cry from the God depicted in the more ancient Jewish scriptures. The point is not that God changes, but that our conceptions of the divine do.

does? Can we let God just be YHVH—can we live with the idea of letting God simply BE?

V BUILDING A GOD-CONCEPT

Once I got to this point in my thinking, I realized that it is not YHVH from whom I am seeking an explanation for suffering, but rather from my ancestors' perception of God that I inherited as a child and embraced as a young man. However, until I fully embraced YHVH's mystery, I stood spiritually conflicted, with part of me still clinging to traditional image of God and thus ready to argue and protest, and another part of me in the process of sloughing off this too-tight theological skin.

A Presbyterian Christian colleague, Daniel Migliore, visited Seattle University's School of Theology and Ministry in 2000 as a scholar-in-residence.[15] When we were first introduced, he jumped up upon hearing my name, happily shocked to meet me in person. I was just puzzled. Then he gave me an inscribed copy of his book, *Rachel's Cry*, and only after I had read it did I realize why he had been excited to meet me—we were fellow travelers on a lonely theological road that advocated protest as a form of prayer.[16]

I told him that despite the fact that I rejected many of the accoutrements of the traditional God, I could not let completely go of this old supernatural God-concept of my ancestors. I was both wrestling with and releasing God at the same time and I was confused. "Anson," he asked, "why do you need to resolve it? What's wrong with living with contradiction?" Ultimately his advice freed me up to move in new theological directions.

In the course of my spiritual development, I moved away from the biblical concept of a caring, supernatural God who intervenes in history and in individual human lives (the moved Mover) to a philosophically

15. Now professor emeritus of theology at Princeton Theological Seminary.

16. Billman and Migliore, *Rachel's Cry*. Another Christian thinker who also is exploring this path, albeit from an evangelical position, is Dan Allender. In his books *Cry of the Soul* (coauthored with Tremper Longman III) and *The Healing Path*, he develops an evangelical Christian basis for prayers of protest as a path towards emotional and spiritual healing. More recently have come Morrow's *Protest Against God* and Mandolfo's *God in the Dock* and *Daughter Zion Talks Back*. Beside these good people are my Jewish fellow-travelers, or rather, my fellow trailblazers: Blumenthal, author of *Facing the Abusing God*; Boteach, *Wrestling with the Divine*; Weiss, *Pious Irreverence*; and Jacobs, *Rethinking Jewish Faith*.

based God who still intervenes (the unmoved Mover), to a deist concept of a God who exists but does not intervene (the unmoved Unmover), and now am weighing the possibility of a God who is empathetic but inactive (the moved Unmover). As I distinguish between YHVH and these human constructs of God, I am forced to admit that I have ideas that I impose on YHVH's ineffability too. Yet even so, I find myself building a God-concept.

What does my emerging God-concept look like?

As always, I start from the ground up, with what I experienced and what I believe to be real. From my most significant spiritual experience, I intuit that YHVH is somehow an actual Presence. But since I cannot verify this, I can only go so far as to say that I want, need, and even choose to conceive of God in this way.

To begin with, I acknowledge that my God-concept is built on the bedrock of primeval experiences of the divine. Humbly, I suggest that my experience of the divine was no different than those that motivated Avraham, Moshe, and others to speak and act as they did. But the Abrahamic faiths are the product of an ancient mindset in which God was perceived to speak directly to individuals and to act through natural and historical events.[17] Their perceptions of the world and the divine-human relationship are different than mine—although many people in these faiths today believe that God continues to act in this same way—and I accept this.

In order to liberate God, as it were, from this ancient God-concept, it helped me to compare a typical Abrahamic religion to the human developmental process. We all know that children process information differently than do adults and that they understand God and faith and other theological concepts differently than do adults.[18] Why not apply the same principle to our collective spiritual experiences to allow for change over the millennia? Perhaps our monotheistic concepts of God represent a collective human developmental process akin to how each of us grows and learns. Paralleling a child's sense of faith, many religions have been based on the

17. James Kugel in his book *The Great Shift* posits that biblical characters—Abraham, for example—shared a common worldview with Homer's heroes, one in which God or gods spoke directly with people, motivating their behavior. Julian Jaynes, in his book *The Origins of Consciousness*, suggests that in preconscious times "the gods" spoke to everyone, but he hypothesizes that human brains have actually changed over time. As time passed and self-consciousness emerged, only those few, like the prophets, who retained or cultivated a "bi-cameral" mind were viewed as being directly in touch with the divine will. Or maybe it is all in the cultural context?

18. See for example Fowler, *Stages of Faith*.

existence of a God or gods who function as a supernatural parent (for better and for worse). I think it is bred into our very beings, particularly at certain stages of individual life and in certain types of civilization, to view God in this way. The fact that many people today still embrace this biblical type of god demonstrates its timeless continuing appeal, proving that there is no progressive evolution with regards to God-concepts. An individual may go through various stages of faith and s/he may find a comfortable spiritual home at any stage, never finding a need to move on, or s/he may continue to search and seek a better resting place with a different sense of the divine.

Similarly, God-concepts may change to fit the times and the general outlook of a particular era. A rabbinic colleague, Rav Soloff, has delineated some possible connections between human self-perception and a God-concept as follows:

> When man's world was the size of a family, his creator and su-preme authority, his God could be an ancestor. When man's world was his clan, his creator and supreme authority, his God could be a patriarch. When man's world was his nation, his creator and su-preme authority, his God could be a king. And when vast empires arose to rule over scores of kingdoms, prophets came to believe that there was One God, the King of Kings . . .
>
> In most recent centuries man's astronomical world has ex-ploded to encompass billions of years and myriads of universes, while his "tangible" world has imploded to infinitesimal particles and incomprehensible dimensions . . .
>
> In this new century "God" can no longer be imagined as the biblical Creator/King and Lawgiver/Savior, His Word revealed in human speech, never to be reinterpreted. God must be understood as Unlimited, beyond human imagination.[19]

It cannot be stressed enough that there is no sense of progress in our per-ceptions of the divine. Our views about God are no better or no worse than previous ones. It is just about our changing perceptions of God. And all

---

19. Email. See also Soloff, "My God." Another rabbinic colleague, Daniel Schiff, in "Reimagining Torah" proposes a metaphor which sees "Torah as the early life devel-opment of the Jewish personality," noting that the Torah offers critical foundational knowledge that shapes how Jews see and feel the world, and it provides the earliest lessons regarding the primary relationships of self, family, and God. Still playing with the concepts of growth, development, and relationship, but this time seeing them from God's perspective, as it were, one could consider Torah to be the *Portrait of Yahweh as a Young God*, as the humorous title of a book by Greta Wels-Schon puts it, or as Jack Miles describes in *God: A Biography*.

these God-concepts flourish together, both in the past and in the present, as individuals and generations discover and imagine on their own.

But the assumption that underlies all these diverse God-concepts, and which has sustained the Jewish people's faith down through the centuries, is that all these God-concepts represent one and the same Being, YHVH.[20] This same assumption also sustains Christianity, Islam, and other Abrahamic faiths and the various God-concepts each has developed and maintained over the centuries. Furthermore, just as contemporary Jewish ideas about God are related to other late-twentieth/early-twenty-first-century ideas of God and spirituality being articulated by contemporaries of other faiths around the world, so too previous Jewish ideas of God influenced and were influenced by the religious environments and civilizations in which they were developed. All our ideas about the divine are interrelated; all are one, if we choose to see them as such—wheels within wheels, as Yehezkiel (Ezekiel) would say, and all part of a greater Whole.

Because I am a Jew, I *choose* to view YHVH/God primarily through a Jewish lens.[21] Beyond what I have imbibed from the well of Jewish tradition are the ideas I have gleaned from the study of other faiths and through personal reflection. All of these influence my conception of "the living God." My relationship with God runs both horizontally in the present across space and also vertically through time. Spatially, my relationship with YHVH occurs within the context of the North American Jewish relationship with God, which occurs within the context of the general North American religious experience, which occurs within the context of the late-twentieth/early-twenty-first-century world religious experience. Temporally, my relationship with YHVH is also related to Jewish God-concepts of the European Enlightenment *and* to a Hasidic Jew's view of God in

20. I take my inspiration for this idea from *Anim Zemirot*, the so-called Hymn of Glory, a mystical poem-prayer composed by Yehudah HeHasid (the Pious), who died in 1217. This assumption is indirectly affirmed in the thrice-daily recitation of the Sh'ma, the core prayer of Judaism (which in fact is not a prayer at all, but a reminder): "Hear, O Yisrael; YHVH is our God, YHVH is One." While most people assume this to mean we worship only one God (who also happens to be the "true" God), it also asserts that all our various ways of conceiving God are one too: "Hear, O Yisrael; that which we call YHVH is our God, all our ideas of YHVH are One."

21. My teacher Jordan Paper expressed the connection between his own mystical experience and Judaism in this way: "In my own case in this regard, my experience of Nothingness is real, not a matter of belief, and since, along with other Abrahamic mystics, I assume this is the God of others so experienced, I will take this experience as the experience of God, when I am thinking in Jewish terms."

eighteenth-century Eastern Europe *and* a Chinese Jew's sense of God in the seventeenth century; to a Sephardic Jew's conception of God in medieval Muslim Spain *and* a Judean's understanding of God in the first century of the Common Era *and* an ancient Israelite's perception of God in the fourth century before the Common Era. All very different ways of looking at God, to be sure, but all somehow related, the earlier all influencing the latter, with the contemporary built upon all its predecessors, and all influencing me.

Because of my Jewish cultural context and my own personal preferences, if and when I choose to endow YHVH with any qualities at all, they would be those qualities that Jews (and others) traditionally have believed God to have and which I still value, primarily because they are what I want to implement in my life and in this world: first and foremost, the attributes of justice and mercy, compassion, love, and accessibility. If I were building a God-concept that, miraculously, could actually become God, ideally I'd want to imbue my God with all these fine qualities.

At the same time, however, there are many other traditional qualities that trouble me, specifically those based around the concept of a supernatural God—a God who exists above, beyond, and outside Creation. Associated with this concept of a supernatural God are qualities that I reject as contrary to my experience, repugnant, or archaic: first and foremost, that God is omnipotent and omniscient; second, that God has the ability to intervene in history and/or in individual lives; third, images of God as male, a warrior, king, judge, punitive father, or husband; and fourth, peripherals such as the angelic court. These attributes may be no more or less valid than the ones I prefer. The only real difference is that the latter do not speak to me, mostly because my historical and cultural context is so different from the ones in which these attributes originally were developed.

All these attributes are a problem for me because of how petitionary prayer doesn't work; they are a problem because of unwarranted suffering in our world; they are a problem because I think a supernatural God belongs to an era in which the earth was at the center of the universe, as flat as a pancake, with the sky as a solid hemisphere above and heaven—with God enthroned—beyond that. In the beginning, this God and his hosts competed with the gods of other nations; then, having vanquished them, He derided them as idols; and finally, God and his heavenly host reigned supreme and unassailable for centuries, until the modern era, when the scientific/philosophical assault on theism began. But, as John Shelby Spong has pointed out, theism and God are not the same.[22] Theism is but one definition of God and, in my opinion, its time is done. For me, that God is dead; but YHVH is and shall be.

What about female imagery to describe God? A friend, Marla Meislin, strongly challenged my basic assumptions about God that serve as the foundation of this book. On the one hand, she said, there is a vibrant, clearly articulated interaction with "the big G" (my term of endearment, not hers) based on my male images of God. On the other hand, she observed that in all other ways I am an (idiosyncratically) observant and committed Jew. Could it be, she suggested ever so gently, that the Jewish home life and values I cherish were inculcated and nurtured in me by the women in my life—my mother, my aunts, and grandmother—and that this was the hidden source both for my moments with the gentle Presence and for focusing on compassion as a primary value? Had she known the Hebrew, she probably would have asked me where the *r-kh-m* רחם ("womb") was in my concept of compassion (*rakhamim*"). She certainly had a point.[23]

I empathize with other feminists about the generally harsh, judgmental, male God imagery and gender bias that predominate in the Abrahamic traditions. I too am greatly troubled by it, but it is hard to say what bothers me more: the male authority figure imagery or simply that imagery is used at all. Imagery is a problem not just because it creates images in our minds and thus limits YHVH, but also because imagery is ambiguous. God as "Father" may constitute a loving, protective image for one person; a savage, brutal image for another.

---

22. Spong, *Why Christianity Must Change or Die*, chapters 3 and 4 in particular.

23. I must acknowledge, where I hadn't before, the role that women have played in my spiritual development. My formative Jewish experiences were those I love the most to this day: observance at home of Shabbat and the holy days. All this was the domain of my mother and my aunts. My mother also made sure the entire family—even my reluctant father—attended synagogue as often as possible, at least on Friday nights and holidays. In her own way, she was quite devout, a Jewish mix of the traditional and the revolutionary. My mother always had incredibly high performance standards, which she applied to God as well as to her children. I distinctly remember her muttering under her breath during worship about theological ideas with which she disagreed. It was my mother's spiritual and intellectual passion that fueled my own drive; my father, otherwise religiously unengaged, modeled behavior that was less inquisitive but also less judgmental. I also must tip my hat (or *kippah*) to each of my wives, for they too, each in her own way, added immeasurably to my spiritual growth in the course of our years together.

These are precisely the same problems I also have with female imagery associated with God.[24] For me, describing YHVH with female imagery in addition to male ones only compounds the problem of using imagery in the first place. Both are equally offensive because they limit and confine our conceptions of YHVH. (Being an iconoclast is hell.) So, if I don't address God as "Father," "King," or "Judge," I also won't address God as "Mother" or even by such gender-neutral terms as "Parent" or "Ruler"—and don't even get me started about the *sefirot*, the divine emanations of classical Jewish mysticism. The idea of God as Father, Mother, or Parent no longer works for me. Terms such as these say far more than I am willing or able to say about YHVH, because for me YHVH transcends gender and gender roles. "Creator" I can live with.

Paradoxically, inanimate God imagery bothers me far less because no one is going to confuse God with being a Rock, a Light, a Fortress, etc. Everyone knows these are only metaphors. But, given my reticence to talk about God, I have no real need of appealing metaphors and similes with which to describe God. To describe YHVH in any way is a form of image-making and, as a radical monotheist, I prefer just to let YHVH Be.

Nonetheless, when my friend, the late Mary Dougherty, described her vision of the divine-human relationship as "God as she, a mother or—even better—a grandmother, who has created us, reared us, given us role models (like Jesus) and set us on our collective and individual ways; and now that we are grown up, really wants us to succeed, and grieves with and for us when we don't," I have to admit to a certain deeply felt longing. My heart yearns for such an intimate sense of connection and relationship with God as she describes; my head, however, says that this imagery presumes far too much. To keep the peace between my body parts, I listen to both and strive to be content living with this contradiction until, if ever, I know differently.[25]

---

24. In traditional Jewish religious thought, feminine images associated with God are all based on God being seen as male. It should be noted that most of these feminine aspects are nouns with feminine endings in Hebrew, as if to say that their gender is predicated on their grammar. Some of the more common consorts are: the *Shekhinah*, or God's feminine presence that dwells on earth (paralleling God, our Father in heaven); *Shabbat*, the Sabbath Queen or Bride, a personification of the seventh day; *Hochmah*, a personification of Wisdom; Torah, not just the book but a metaphysical entity that God consulted in creating the world; *Yisrael*, the personification of the Jewish people, married to God; and *Yerushalayim /Tziyyon*, personifications of Jerusalem and the land of Zion.

25. Jay Michaelson in *Everything Is God*, 106–8, offers an intriguing alternative, calling imagery "masks" that we can put on God in order to better relate to That Which Cannot Be Named.

I now consider God to be much more of a mystery than I ever did, so the qualities traditionally ascribed to God bother me less because I know they are only human attributions of God; our projections onto God, not actually God. I have also "forgiven" God for all that has been and still is wrong in our world—in other words, I have let go of traditional perceptions of God and let go of the issue of divine providence in order to let God simply be YHVH. Of the traditional God I could still have expectations, but I expect *nothing* of YHVH other than to be aware of YHVH's presence, and this feels right for me. I am willing to let God just be the Name, YHVH, the One who will be what the One will be, the One who can be tasted and perceived.[26]

Based on my personal experience, I feel YHVH's omnipresence is real—it is the only "omni" I accept—*precisely because have I experienced it.* I feel that YHVH is somehow present everywhere and in everything, and a bit of that Presence resides in every living person, animating every living creature and even, perhaps, our entire planet as well. I view Creation not as a machine, but as organisms within organisms, worlds within worlds, a living whole, and I have come to realize that my concept of YHVH does not extend beyond the circle of life that comprises our planet. (Pending future discoveries, the rest of the universe seems lifeless.) But with regards to our planet—the place of Creation—here I choose to think that YHVH somehow both infuses everything with "the breath of life" and at the same time transcends everything with "Presence." (I say this without knowing exactly what I mean, but I do intuit it.) Scholars call this conception of God panentheism and, although it is only a theological concept, not reality, it appeals to me, in part because it allows me to retain and build upon the foundations of my people's sacred stories and traditions.[27]

What I am able to affirm is that, based on the name YHVH, God represents the infusion of constant creativity into the world, which in turn gives all living things the possibility and the power to live and grow—and, yes, to decline and die—both individually and collectively. YHVH is the animating force of all life, the living dynamic of all that exists, the source both of what we perceive as good and also what we perceive as bad. That is what radical monotheism means.

26. Teh/Ps 34:8. For an introduction to the study of the mystical experience, see Paper, *Mystic Experience*.

27. See Green, *Seek My Face, Speak My Name*; Borg, *God We Never Knew*; and Bass, *Grounded*. Spong, in *Why Christianity Must Change or Die*, calls his non-theistic God "the Ground of Being."

On the other hand, based on my spiritual experience, I also feel that YHVH can be experienced primarily as a force for good because for a brief delicious moment in my life I was able to tap into the sensations of peace, love, and joy that derived from my sense of connection with the divine. [28] My dilemma is that I yearn to know unequivocally that YHVH tilts life to the side of positive potentiality, but I go back and forth on this issue, unable to take it on faith.

Daniel Migliore described my flailing leap of faith more accurately and articulately than I ever could because, while I was busy flailing, he was observing my trajectory:

> Unless I misunderstand the thrust of your book, you imply that when we do justice and love mercy we are somehow in harmony with the divine presence. We are, as it were, living "with the grain of the universe," to use a phrase of Stanley Hauerwas. Conversely, when we act unjustly or suffer injustice, such acts and sufferings are not in accordance with God's intentions; they run against the grain of the universe as created by God.[29]

His words remind me of a phrase often attributed to Martin Luther King: "The arc of the moral universe is long but it bends toward justice."[30] Some may call this providence in operation and even for me, skeptic that I am, it does seem operational—and if it isn't, I will take it on the hope that it is. (It is far better than the alternative.) When I look at history, I see that empires that greatly abuse people eventually always fall, and this gives me hope. True, much suffering may happen during the historical experience of delayed justice—and there is much unfortunate injustice in that delay—but justice does seem to come eventually. This is the triumph of the Exodus hope over historical experience. To me this suggests that life tilts toward "the good" and "the blessing."

28. My friend and former colleague in hospice chaplaincy Joyce Greenberg, a Jewish Daoist, takes exception to my belief in the concept of positive change. Her view, in my words, is that however much life appears to change, it is really always in balance. I, on the other hand, believe that life's changes are dynamic—hopefully and eventually for the better.

29. Email.

30. Words to this effect were originally penned by Theodore Parker, a Unitarian minister, Transcendentalist, and abolitionist. In 1857 he published a collection of ten sermons, the third of which was entitled "Of Justice and Conscience," which contained these words: "Look at the facts of the world. You see a continual and progressive triumph of the right. I do not pretend to understand the moral universe, the arc is a long one, my eye reaches but little ways . . . But from what I see I am sure it bends towards justice."

Being alert to the presence of YHVH in life means seeing the "Presence" everywhere and in everything. I see all life as an extension of YHVH because life is the perpetual re-creation of new possibilities or potentialities. In the natural world, this process apparently is neither good nor bad; it is simply life growing and adapting in seemingly endless variation of itself, like the growth that goes on in our own bodies, with our cells replacing themselves continuously, oblivious to our conscious existence and will.

Having an awareness of this Presence means, at the very least, that when I look at other living things I strive to recognize the existence of a shared divine dimension. They are no less than we: unique particles, or moments, of life's slow unfolding. On the basis of this principle alone, we ought to treat other living creatures with a degree of reverence, even those we choose to eat.[31]

I see YHVH's presence in each individual's maturation process; that which begins at the start of life is the potential for good, for positive change and growth, for improvement and development. For me, the clearest manifestation of this process has been seeing loved ones grow from oblivious infancy to the point when they can interact with other people, when they reach out with the all the sweet innocence that only the very young have and begin to build actual relationships with those around them. I also see this positive exercise of potentiality as youth seizes hold of maturity and ventures out into the world, when two people find love together, and when a baby is born.

I think the exercise of positive potentiality is more consciously applied in human creativity, from commonplace simple things, like how we dress ourselves or how we decorate our dwellings, to the grander outbursts of creative expression, as when an artist plays with color and shape, or when a musician builds sound upon sound, or when a writer weaves words into narratives or poetry. And I think that this power of positive potentiality resides most particularly in our doing good deeds, when we care for one another, even to the point of death and beyond. All these are acts that add to the positive energy among us.

To be sure, my soul stirs to the idea of a God who somehow actually shares our fate and participates in our journeys,[32] and I realize that

31. This is one of the rationales for keeping kosher.

32. In both Judaism and Christianity, it is taught that God somehow shares our pain and that what we do "affects" God. This empathic, suffering but, ultimately active God is as much a traditional Jewish concept of God as it is obviously a Christian one. In some midrashim, God feels pain when Israel suffers in exile, mourns, weeps, acts as one who

to hold this belief could be very comforting. Knowing that somehow God shares what we are going through when we feel distress can fuel our inner spiritual reserves, enabling us to struggle along with renewed energy. Having such a God would also pass my Holocaust litmus test because such a God could be a source of personal comfort and support in Auschwitz but without the expectation that God would actively intervene. But I cannot say with certainty that God suffers when we do, or that God celebrates or is energized when we choose a higher, nobler path in our actions. YHVH may somehow "care" (to put it in human terms) or may somehow "participate" in what we do, but I don't really *know* this to be the case. All I know is that I experienced a benign—dare I say loving—Presence. So I set this idea of an empathic God aside even as I yearn to know it is real.[33] Perhaps someday I may be blessed with this knowledge, perhaps not—but it is not something I am currently willing to take on faith.

A Presence, perhaps with a hint of personality, who/that provides positive potentiality to life—this is a job description for a deity?! Not by many people's standards, but it works for me. YHVH is there to be experienced, not to do our bidding, and that is why I assert: "I know there is a God, I just don't know what S/He/It does." Nowadays, I rarely choose to speak about

---

is ill, even is led into exile with his people. See my *Arguing with God*, 83 and texts referenced there. Consider also this beautiful teaching from the *Zohar* Bamidbar 118a/b: "In all deeds it behooves a person to imitate the celestial model, and to realize that according to the nature of a deed below there is a responsive stirring on high." One of my favorite passages from the Christian Bible (after deleting the harsh section on hellfires) is Matthew 25:34–45, which makes this same connection. See also Fretheim, *Suffering of God*.

33. Here is what my friend Shoshana Brown had to say about this yearning:

> Certainly it would matter to me if I could have proof that there is an Ultimate Intelligence Who is Listening. That would matter to me a lot—even if this Being were not able to "do" anything to respond to my prayers or to any of the world's problems, except listen. But since this proof is lacking, I wonder instead if it matters whether I "believe" there is a God Who Listens, or, being short on belief, whether it is enough that I pour out my words to God anyway—not because of my "faith," but because of my irrepressible need to direct my heart's greatest concerns and devotion toward something, someOne, not limited by time and space . . . God is said to be omnipresent—and I want to believe this. So I act as if I do—in spite of all the difficulties. I am careful not to expect God to "fix" things—either in the world at large or in my own life. I seek only this: a place to pour out my heart, and the solace that comes from a sense of Presence—even though I know that my desire for this "Presence" may be what creates it.

"God." It is too confusing a term. When people ask me if I believe in God, I say: "First, tell me what you mean by 'God' and what you mean by 'believe,' and then I'll try to answer your question." Rather, I prefer to follow Lao Zi's dictum: "Those who know do not speak; those who speak do not know."[34]

34. Lao Tzu, *Tao Te Ching*, 117.

Chapter 9

Iyov's Theophany II
Unraveling Revelation

"Then YHVH replied to Iyov out of the tempest and said:"
(Iyov 38:1)

I   WHAT IS REVELATION?

IN THE ABRAHAMIC FAITHS, it is impossible to talk about what we think
we know about God without discussing the concept of divine revelation
because it has been through revelation that our ancestors believed God
communicated with them. Revelation—now that is a challenging concept!

Once, when I was asked to teach a class that was studying Torah, it was
my misfortune to have to teach a lesson on a section of *Vayikrah/Leviticus*.
As anyone who has ever read this book of the Torah knows, its focus is on
the rituals of the priesthood, the sacrificial cult, and on ritual purification
of one sort or another. So distinctly detailed is this book that, for many
modern people, it challenges the very concept of divine revelation. After all,
it is hard enough to imagine the God of all Creation revealing anything to
human beings at all, never mind to an obscure band of former slaves on the
run in the middle of the Sinai desert, let alone to focus on such minutiae as
how to offer a sacrifice or what the high priest should wear.

Instead of discussing topics like these, I chose to spend my lesson on the first few words that introduce so many commandments: "And YHVH spoke to Moshe, saying"—and specifically the word "saying." Think about it: What does this word, so commonly and frequently used in the Bible with reference to God, actually mean? With no larynx, lips, or tongue, how does God speak? And if it was not speech as we know it, how did Moshe "hear" these non-words? And how, then, did these non-words become words? And whose words were they? How much was God's revelation and how much was Moshe's (or someone else's) extrapolation? Perhaps God communicated through a dream or by a vision, or perhaps it was an inner voice projected externally? What exactly was the nature of the mystery that we call divine revelation that lies at the heart of the Abrahamic faiths?

II   A DIFFERENT UNDERSTANDING OF REVELATION

After wrestling with the subject of revelation for many years, I came to realize that I needed to let go of the traditional concept of revelation and develop a new theory instead. Let me state at the outset that I do not now believe the revelation to Moshe or any other prophet was supernatural. The problem with a supernatural revelation is that *if* revelation is a miraculous intervention by God into the normal course of human events, *then* there is a basic—and for me unacceptable—contradiction between this phenomenon and the world of experience. Supernatural interventions/miracles are incompatible with the world as I know it, the world made intelligible by scientific method and theory, even though I acknowledge and embrace the mysteries of existence that reside on the borders of what we think we know.[1]

For me, any given revelation must be viewed from the ground up. A revelation is one individual's particular and creative response to what s/he perceives or discerns to be God's call in a specific situation. This means that the words of Torah and the words of the prophets are human responses, not God's utterances, even if they were felt by the prophet and perceived by the people to be divine in origin.[2]

1. My wife, Richelle Harrell, points out that just because I view the world this way doesn't mean that this is how the world actually is. Hindus and Buddhists, for example, posit many worlds and many reincarnations; and science has yet to account for the apparently serendipitous, miraculous, and paranormal events that we all know happen from time to time. And other living creatures have sharper senses than we do and so perceive more than we can. I do not disagree with any of this.

2. Medieval Jewish philosophers, specifically Yehuda HaLevi, author of the *Kuzari*,

We give short shrift to the human role in determining the fate of any given "revelation." For example, in the Bible there were many prophets beyond those whose words we retained; some were "true" and some "false." What happened to their words? The answer is that the words of some, though "true," were lost; others, though "false," were saved; and still others perceived over time as "false" were discarded. What we are left with—what we call the Bible—are revelations' remnants cobbled together and written down by human hands,[3] and what the Tanakh provides are snapshots of the commandments—and of the Jewish perception of the people's relationship with YHVH—at the particular point in time when they were transcribed. Thus our ancient and revered holy texts tell us more about our ancestors' ideas of God and their worldview than they do of the mystery that is God.

Centuries later, the scribes and rabbis decided which books were to be included in the Hebrew Bible and which were excluded, what the order of the books should be, and how to vocalize and thus understand more obscure passages of "God's Word." Antiquity bestowed an ever-increasing holiness to the text itself. Even back at the beginning of the Common Era, some of these texts had been around in some form for fifteen hundred to two thousand years. Two thousand years is not a huge amount of time per se, but for human beings this meant going back almost to the dawn of known history. Materials that old acquire reverence. Ultimately sanctity came to be ascribed to the very words of themselves.[4]

Similarly, at the core of nearly every faith sit sacred stories and sacred teachings. Being human, we all did the same thing with these originally oral transmissions—we first committed them to memory and then we wrote them down. Until we did this, the stories and teachings remained alive, fluid, breathing; they were works in progress. But once the material was written down and age bestowed upon it a certain sanctity, then it became set, as it were, in stone. My friend Sol Ezekiel in fact likened this process to "ossification"—the hardening of soft tissue into a bone-like formation. When a text assumes near-divine status itself, then, in many religious

---

attempted to show that the revelation at Sinai was verifiable since, unlike later (and competing) revelations, the entire Jewish nation participated in it and witnessed it.

3. See Fishbane, *Text and Texture*, xiii.

4. Over the centuries, we Jews have emerged not only as long-time monotheists but also as long-time bibliolators, or book worshippers. We may have given God to the world, but we kept a tighter clasp on the Torah. The physical Torah scroll and the presence of God became all but synonymous in Jewish worship. Furthermore, the same principle of sanctity eventually was applied to the Talmud and even to the prayer book. It was not for nothing that Muslims called us the "People of the Book."

traditions, it becomes blasphemous to suggest that the events and laws in that holy text ever happened otherwise. And once such texts have been enshrined as religious truths, they also serve as a foundation for the institutional religious edifices built upon them—think, for example, of the Catholic Christian Church, the cosmos, and Galileo. The texts and the institutions end up being as sanctified as the root experience/revelation that initially galvanized their creation.

Nor are we today immune from this tendency to sanctify documents. Consider the American Constitution. Like the Torah, the Constitution is valued because its origin goes back to America's very beginnings; it defines America both for Americans and for other nations. As with rabbis and the Torah, constitutional scholars sometimes attempt to determine—but actually project their views onto—the intent of the Founding Fathers. Consider also how we revere and preserve the physical document known as the Constitution—it is the modern equivalent of storing the tablets of the Law in the Temple! Imagine how the Constitution and the Founding Fathers who drafted it will be regarded in, say, one thousand or two thousand years from now.[5]

However, if you acknowledge that revelations are limited by time and place yet still resonate with value and meaning, then they retain much of their worth as "timeless" teachings—"God's own words," as it were. I do no disservice to the messenger or the message when I assert that revelation is a human response to a perceived experience of the divine. What matters in the end is that the revelatory experience transformed the messenger and resulted in his/her transmitting something of profound, life-changing importance to the people of his/her time and to humanity ever after.

How much simpler relating to the Tanakh, New Testament, Qur'an, and other holy texts would be—not to mention the "answers" they are assumed by some to provide on contemporary hot issues such as gender roles, homosexuality, end of life, capital punishment, and many other matters—if we could accept them as human products of particular times and places. We would feel much freer about how we evaluate various stories and commandments, even though we could still regard the texts as repositories of great insight, which also have been imbued with the additional wisdom of subsequent generations. But however divinely inspired we may think them

5. Jill Lepore draws the comparison between constitutional originalists and Christian fundamentalist readings of the Bible, and contrasts those who view the Constitution as a human document with those who enshrine it as divinely inspired, in her article "The Commandments."

to be, they are nonetheless human documents evincing attitudes about God and society from ancient times!

I now view the Jewish holy books as testaments to the continuing and evolving encounter—or, as the name Yisrael suggests, the ongoing struggle—of the Jewish people to relate to its perceptions of God, YHVH. As of this writing, the collective Jewish experience is about four thousand years in the making and Torah probably has been told, adapted, recorded, interpreted, and commented upon for at least three thousand of those years. That we have such an ancient sacred text, that it is accompanied by several millennia of commentary representing the best wisdom of the ages, testifies to the power of the mystery that lies at its heart. And that is why I too continue to mine the Torah (and Jewish tradition) for insights that give meaning, purpose, and value to my life.

III   THE RELATIVITY OF REVELATION

For Jews, Sinai is the quintessential revelatory experience. (For Christians, Muslims, Sikhs, Baha'is, and Latter Day Saints, revelations occurred much later.) According to the Torah itself, Moshe and people received both *mitzvot* (commandments) and a revelatory experience.[6] But who received what and how much? Inquiring rabbinic minds wanted to know.

The ancient rabbis discussed which of the 613 commandments God gave directly to the entire people. One midrash stated that everyone heard everything, but each in his or her own way.[7] Another midrash asserted that God gave the Big Ten, and Moshe the remaining 603. Yet another suggested that God gave the first two of the Ten directly and Moshe the remainder,[8] because if one affirms the first two (I, YHVH, am your God and none else; Do not worship images), then all the rest follow; but if one cannot accept the first two commandments, then the whole Covenant falls apart. Ultimately, in rabbinic thinking, the revelation came to include not only the entire Written Torah (both the commandments and the narrative text) but

6. There is some discrepancy between the accounts of Shem/Exod 20:15–18 and *Dev/Deut* 5:19–28.

7. *Shemot/Exodus Rabbah* 5:9.

8. *b. Makkot* 24a and Horayot 8a. In support of this theory, when the Ten Commandments are chanted in the synagogue according to the upper trope, each commandment is treated as a separate verse, regardless of length. But the first two commandments are combined as one to remind listeners of the "original" revelation—and possibly to enable them to spiritually re-enact the moment of the giving of Torah.

also the Oral Torah (later rabbinic interpretations and adaptations). According to these same rabbis, both were believed to have been given by God to Moshe at Sinai.[9] With this belief, the rabbis of Judaea and the Parthian/Sassanid empires who developed the Oral Torah were able to confirm the rabbinic role as the sole, divinely authorized interpreters of God's word—a very neat trick indeed![10] But, of course, their claim was disputed by the Karaite Jewish sect, by Christianity, and by Islam.

However, centuries later, and from a totally different part of the world, there came a profound—and perhaps humorously playful—Hasidic commentary that elaborates a more mystic interpretation. This particular Hasidic teaching states that God directly uttered *only* the first letter of the first commandment—an *aleph*—a letter that just happens to be a silent letter! Although the rabbis traditionally held that everything Moshe taught came directly from God (and also everything they taught as well!), this teaching has God speak only the following directly to the entire nation: "_____."[11] I may not have God's words exactly right: it may be "_____" or it may be "_____"—it's hard to tell when God speaks silently. For me, this teaching confirms what I think revelation is all about: It has to do with experiencing YHVH being present; it's not about content.

If revelation is an experience of the divine Presence—and the content is something human beings add subsequently—then it is important to differentiate between the two.[12] By separating the experience from the content, we can both "free" God from the chains of past perceptions and look at the content of a revelation more objectively.

9. There is a famous midrash in *b.* Menachot 29b about Moshe being granted the opportunity by God to visit Rabbi Akiva's *yeshiva* (academy). Moshe grows more and more anxious as he hears the master and his disciples expound on Jewish law until Rabbi Akiva declares that what he is teaching "is a law given to Moshe at Sinai."

10. However, there is no such thing as Jewish *textual* fundamentalism. Even though every jot and tittle of the Torah was believed to be the very word of God, it all is subject to human (i.e., rabbinic) interpretation, beginning with the very first letter of the first word and going on from there.

11. My teacher Arthur Lagawier first shared this teaching with me. He probably learned it from his Hasidic grandfather but the teaching originated with the Hasidic Rabbi Mendl Torum of Rymanov (d. 1814). His comment is based on the *Zohar* (II:85b), which states that this *aleph* contained the whole Torah. See Arthur Green, *Seek My Face*, 115–17.

12. Apparently I'm in good company in making this differentiation. Franz Rosenzweig wrote that "the Lord spoke" signifies the end of revelation and the beginning of interpretation, while Abraham Joshua Heschel viewed the Torah as "a minimum of revelation and a maximum of interpretation." See Sommer, *Revelation and Authority*.

Traditionally, different faiths have transformed the revelatory experience into content, either as primarily commandments (in the case of Judaism), or as belief (in the case of Christianity based on Paul's vision of Jesus), or both (in the case of Islam). The great scandal of the Abrahamic faiths has been their intolerance not only of non-monotheistic faiths, but also of each other and of internal dissent: Jew versus idolater, Christian versus Jew, Muslim against Hindu, Christian against Muslim, Catholic versus Protestant, Orthodox versus Reform Jew, Sunni versus Shia (and even Hindu against Buddhist and Buddhist against Muslim). What terrible deeds have been done—and continue to be done—in the name of God and religion![13]

Just as Judaism differentiated itself from the religions of Egypt and Canaan by disparaging them (in God's name), so too, as Christianity and Islam developed, each in turn asserted its claim to supersede its predecessor as God's chosen while its predecessor denounced the new faith as heresy. This trend has continued with other faiths since then.[14] But why would God need to update revelation from time to time? One revelation ought to have been enough. However, if one considers revelation from the human side, then there is always a need for revision and reform because the receptor and implementer is a limited creature made of flesh and blood, here today and gone tomorrow. Our experiences perpetually call out for new understandings of what we think God "asks" of us.

Indeed, every Abrahamic faith tradition "hears God" in unique and distinct ways. Within each faith, every generation and every individual discovers—or rediscovers—God and purpose, just as they do sex, love, loss, birth, and death. The experience historically called "revelation" is replicable everywhere; every place and every age has its sages, male and female. If the revelatory experience is a sort of spiritual insight or enlightenment, then it all depends on one's aptitude, preparation, expectations, level of spiritual development, and the lens through which one looks at life. Each perception is unique, distinct, and valid, but all represent all-too-human responses to a revelatory experience of some kind. Our understandings of the ultimate reality and of our place in the universe complement one another, precisely because that reality is ultimately unknowable and the infinite whole will always be greater than the sum of its many parts.[15]

13. Two wonderful condemnations of religion, specifically the Abrahamic ones, are: Harris, *End of Faith* and Hitchens, *God Is Not Great*.

14. Muslims consider the Baha'i faith as heretical and many Christians likewise take a dim view of the Church of Jesus Christ of Latter Day Saints.

15. My wife, Richelle Harrell, challenges me from her perspective as a woman who

This perception applies not just to my contemporaries, but also to those writers and doers of deeds in many lands and many ages, of many faiths and many cultures. All our perceptions are one, transcending time and place, different though they may be. To elaborate on another image I used earlier: Our ideas of God, our religious civilizations, our understanding of our obligations, and indeed our very lives are like coral. We, the living, represent the uppermost tip of a great reef that grows continually, building upon the concepts of previous generations and adding our own ideas to their foundation before we too pass away. There is no progress in this simile, only one generation building on the perceptions and lives of its predecessors while reaching toward the light.

I think that the solution to the conflicting claims of our different faiths lies first in distinguishing religion from the spiritual experience. The former ought to be seen as a *particular* cultural expression of a *universal* human experience, which is the latter. Our religions are the distinctive clothing we wear over our naked human spirituality. Because this experience is a human response to a perceived divine call, then myriad responses are possible. They can be as diverse as our languages, as multiple as there are people. Again, I turn to midrash for inspiration and support. The rabbis taught that every Jew at Sinai heard the Torah being given in a distinct and personal way: young men one way, old men another, women a third way, and children a fourth—even the yet-to-be-born heard it in a special way.[16] Rabbi Shmuel Eliezer Edeles (Maharsha)[17] taught that the entire nation of six hundred thousand people received the Torah at Sinai in order to teach that the Torah has (at least) that many possible interpretations.[18] And if we have so many possible interpretations in just one faith, how much the more so when we consider many faiths and all humanity? Thus another midrash teaches that when God revealed the Torah, his voice split into seven voices and then those seven voices split into all the seventy languages of the world so that everyone could hear and understand.[19]

Once I had let go of my inherited perceptions of God and my too parochial view of revelation, I found I could engage with people of other

practices yoga and meditation: "You say reality is ultimately unknowable, but if a person achieves enlightenment, then there is a complete and total perception of the whole of existence." It may be so, but I can only speak from where I am as a limited and far-from-enlightened man.

16. *Shemot/Exodus Rabbah* 5:9 and *Pesikta d'Rav Kahana*, Piska 12:25.

17. Eastern Europe, 1555–1631.

18. Sacks, "Bamidbar (5768)."

19. *Midrash Tehillim* 65:6.

faiths in a more genuine way. If we are all viewing different facets of the same divine gemstone and if all our faiths are cultural trappings laid upon our naked spirituality, then what is the point in arguing about whose revelation is truer or whose religious civilization is wiser, greater, or better? If revelation really is about experiencing the ineffable, then accepting this premise conceivably can make our faiths less exclusivist and more tolerant of one another. Rather than asserting that our particular faith's revelation is the truest revelation, we can keep the door open to appreciating similar experiences of people of other faiths and cultures.

Over the centuries, our religious differences have obscured our religious similarities, leading to discrimination, persecution, wars, much death, and needless suffering. We need to make a break with how we have conducted ourselves previously. Perhaps, as with children and parents, religions must separate one from another and grow apart as they develop their own unique messages and accomplishments, but it is a shame and often a horror to see how we have dealt with this process throughout history.

Casting blame for these tragedies is pointless—it is easy to do but so harmful for future relations. The past does have power in the present, but we are not doomed to repeat the past. Each occasion inherits history but also a moment of divine potentiality—an opportunity to let go, forgive, change, and grow—and this can enable us to transcend our pasts. Only then we can begin to build relationships that are new and filled with potential for improvement. Recognizing our interrelatedness, we might realize that to attempt to understand one another better is simultaneously an attempt to better understand ourselves as well as our diverse perceptions of God.

By accepting our human limitations in the knowledge of God, by acknowledging our multiple perspectives on God, and by placing responsibility for the well-being of humanity squarely on our collective shoulders, we can set the stage for human reconciliation, interfaith harmony, spiritual growth, and the healing of our world. It ought to make no difference how one conceives of God or how one celebrates one's rituals because the way in which a person lives should be the same for any genuinely spiritual person: it is the practice of practical spirituality. The proof of one's connectedness with the divine manifests in how one lives and in one's deeds.

Theology aside, it is not that complicated.

Chapter 10

At Home with Death

"Why does he give light to the sufferer / And life to the bitter in spirit; /
To those who wait for death but it does not come, / Who search for it
more than for treasure?"
(Iyov 3:20–21)

I   MY WIFE'S DEATH

In March 2010, Merrily was diagnosed with a relapse of ovarian cancer
after being cancer free for ten years. Or maybe it wasn't a relapse but a new
strain of ovarian cancer that somehow suddenly appeared in her spleen—
the doctors never were sure—but it didn't matter. There was little they could
really do. Eight months later she was dead.

After enduring a couple of *pro forma* rounds of chemotherapy, Merrily
decided to forgo further treatments because they were only diminishing
her quality of life. When it became clear that she was going to die, Merrily and I discussed hospice and decided it was the right path for her to
take. Hospice meant the end of tortuous chemotherapy; it meant accepting
that death was coming and preparing for it; and it meant she could die at
home rather than in a hospital. Hospice nurses kept Merrily mostly pain
free; hospice social workers and chaplains helped her process feelings and
concerns; my daughters and I, and a few close friends, supported her physically, emotionally, and spiritually. I took several jobs with the flexibility to

work from home and consequently was able to spend most of my wife's final months with her.

Seeing her realm of control shrink from community to house to bedroom, I agreed to have our bedroom done over to her artist's-eye specifications. No hospital bed for her! Instead she chose new bed coverings, drapes, a chandelier, and colored trim—all of which was done in a couple of days, just weeks before she died.

We also went the "Death with Dignity" route. Following the newly instituted Washington State law, we took all the steps necessary to acquire the lethal dosages of the drugs but, oddly enough, just having them in her possession gave Merrily the control and freedom she needed to let go and let nature take its course.

Just before Merrily died, I contacted the Jewish funeral home and tried to arrange for a traditional Jewish ritual cleansing of the body with a few modifications. I didn't want a bonnet on her head—my stylish wife would not have wanted to depart this world looking like a medieval Jewess. I didn't want the women who washed her body to recite psalms; modern Jewish and secular poetry were more to my wife's taste. And I wanted our daughters and a couple of my wife's closest female friends to observe, if not participate in, the ritual washing.

Most important of all: my daughters and I decided to do something highly unusual in this age and place—we wanted the body returned to our home instead of remaining in the mortuary overnight.

In our society, we relegate the task of staying with the body to the funeral home, but I couldn't do it. In a Jewish mortuary setting, a paid or volunteer watchperson has a small room from which s/he can watch and pray over multiple bodies. This suffices the letter of Jewish tradition but falls short in so many other ways. Most significantly, it doesn't honor the power and potency of that time in the mourning process right after the death of a loved one. Someone you love, someone who has been a part of your life for years, dies and the body is taken away immediately, separated from loved ones for hours, not to be seen again? It made no sense—neither to me nor to my daughters.

As it turned out, what we wanted was the deal-breaker for the funeral home. Once a funeral home takes possession of a body, it cannot release it until it is disposed of. What we did instead was intimate, personal, and loving, and a source of great comfort.

II   AFTER HER DEATH

The funeral home director suggested that I contact a women's branch of the *hevra kaddisha* (the group responsible for doing the ritual washing) to arrange for a modified washing ceremony. He told me that its members all belonged to a local Reform congregation, Kol HaNeshamah. I sat up with a jolt. "Of course! How could I have forgotten that!?" I had just finished a year as interim rabbi of that congregation and I had actually helped set up the *hevra kaddisha* program during that time. Nonetheless, in the moment of my distress it had totally escaped my mind. But that is what happens in the midst of intense grief—one doesn't think clearly at all. So I contacted my friend and colleague Zari Weiss, now the rabbi at Kol HaNeshamah, to arrange for the washing and dressing of my wife's body at our home when the time came. To this small group of women I invited my wife's closest and most grounded Jewish friends and our daughters.

Merrily died in her own bed, with me and a caregiver by her side. Her actual death was exactly as the Talmud describes it: "like taking a hair out of milk."[1] Just a sigh and she was gone. Somewhat typical of dying people, she "chose" to die just after both of our daughters had left their vigil to go to their homes for the night. They returned and we sat around the bed, talking and reminiscing, waiting for the funeral home staff and the *hevra kaddisha* women to arrive.

I, as a man, chose to follow the gender-segregating tradition and let these brave, compassionate women care for my wife's body. Behind the closed door of our bedroom, they worked for hours to wash my beloved's body and to dress her in the burial shrouds—minus the bonnet. Jewish law was consulted, but it was used more as a guide than a rulebook for what they did. And, while this was going on, I was embraced by other friends, both male and female, keeping me company in our living room. During this intense period of mourning prior to the funeral, food was eaten, alcohol drunk, tears shed, words of consolation shared—and I felt that Merrily was present too in the midst of it all. It felt good to be cared for while knowing that my wife's body was also being cared for in the other room.

The women put Merrily in a traditional Jewish casket, the plain pine box that the funeral home had delivered, and called me in for a final goodbye. A Japanese-American friend had made some exquisite origami cranes, which we laid around her. A moment of silence, a kiss, and we closed the casket.

1. *b. Berachot* 8a.

With the work done and the house now emptied, my daughters and I sat around the closed casket and chatted. We even watched my wife's favorite movie—J. J. Abram's *Star Trek*—on DVD together with her! It may seem disrespectful to some, but we all felt it was what she would have wanted for her last evening with us.

As we did this vigil together, we were gradually able to accept the fact that my wife/their mother had died. We watched, we checked, we listened. Wishful thinking and heartfelt prayers aside, it was clear that she was really and truly dead. But, perhaps even more significantly, the experience enabled us to linger together for hours. That night, I slept in our bed with her coffin alongside it. I don't recall anything of the experience other than this simple fact.

The next morning, the funeral home attendants returned to transport the body to the cemetery and we accompanied them out. Merrily had not left our home for weeks during her final illness; in her death she remained in our sight and in our presence; now we escorted her out ceremonially to be buried. With family and friends to buoy us up, we went to the graveyard and sent her on her final journey from this world.

Weeks later, when I related this experience to the grief support group I attended through the hospice program, some members were surprised and others moved. Many had been told not to be present when the body was taken away; most felt that they were abandoning their loved one at a crucial moment. Intuitively, I had known that I didn't want to go down that route and, by keeping Merrily's body by our side right up until the funeral, I felt we did right by my wife. Equally important, we did right by us, the living.

Of Merrily's funeral itself, I remember hardly anything other than being surrounded by people who loved and cared for her and for us. Were it not for the recordings made and the copies of the speeches given, I would not remember a word. But I do remember sitting *shiva*[2] in our house.

My God, the house was jammed each and every evening—not to mention a steady stream of family and closer friends during the daytime. The evenings were an ordeal and, as a result, I now prefer to visit mourners during the day when we can sit together and reminisce and chat rather than deal with the crowds that come to pray in the evening. In our case, I did not want to pray, and I certainly was not ready to say *kaddish*[3] yet. Even though

2. The seven-day mourning period during which immediate family members stay at home. Traditionally, friends and community members come each night to recite the evening prayers and comfort the mourners by their presence.

3. A prayer of praise to God that is offered at the end of every Jewish service and

I had had months to prepare for her death, my grief was still too raw and my sense of injustice still too high. Instead I asked people to share stories and we'd conclude each gathering with a Jewish melody. But by the conclusion of the *shiva* period, I was ready to let go and we ended it by reciting the *kaddish* for the first and only time.

Now began the real work of grieving. With no more crowds to "entertain," I was on my own, with only my thoughts to keep me company. I dutifully went to work every day, but did so as an automaton, and when I came home each night and closed the front door, I would howl with a disembodied sound that came from God-knows-where within me. Nights were particularly bad as there were no distractions. Then I would have trouble breathing and my sleep, when it came, was fitful. Life seemed not worth the effort.

I thought a change of scenery might help so I went on visits to my brother and my sister but found that I must have accidentally packed my grief in the suitcase, because no matter where I went, there my grief was too. Returning home only brought out the intensity of my loss more acutely once again. Again, there were even times when death seemed preferable to the pain I felt in my gut. Fortunately, this time round I knew to reach out and share what I was going through, so I l talked my heart out: with family and friends, with a therapist, and in a grief group run by the hospice program. And ever so slowly I began to heal.[4]

III SOME REFLECTIONS

Life as I See It

One of the sad realities of life, it seems to me, is that, although we are social creatures needing intimate relationships, nonetheless we are not truly capable of transcending our physical and emotional distinctiveness. The best we can do is approximate what another person feels based on our own experiences.

We also make the journey through life's stages on our own, individually—although we do like to compare notes. Just as parents cannot spare their children from falling as they learn to walk, so too we all must discover life's

---

particularly by the mourners.

4. Elizabeth Neeld's books *Seven Choices* and *Tough Transitions* helped me a great deal as well.

experiences personally, individually, for ourselves. Although we do learn by watching and observing our parents, families, and friends, there is precious little of life's knowledge that we can actually pass on to our children, so each generation must live its own ignorance and grow its own wisdom even though it might mean repeating the same missteps.[5] Like Sisyphus, one generation acquires knowledge as it rolls its boulder up life's hillside only to see the next generation necessarily repeat the task all over again.

As we live, we learn that loss and grief are natural parts of human existence—would that it were otherwise—but they are as much a part of life as joy and pleasure. From the moment of birth until the day of death, life is made up of innumerable minor losses and a number of great ones, each with its own special grief, just as it is also made of innumerable gains, each with its own special joy.[6] Ultimately, life ends, and with it all that we held dear. As much as we know that death is the expected conclusion of life, even so there is always a shocking sense of loss and a feeling of bewildered abandonment when it actually occurs.

If I were to sum up existence I would say it is this: We are born and live but for a short while in a number of "communities," from family to friends to faith or ethnicity, from neighborhood to city to nation, and even to the world. The groups in which we live and to which we have contributed during our brief existence—these continue on, having been shaped in some way, small or large, by our fleeting presence on this planet. C'est tout.

So how should we deal with these facts: that all experience is personal, individually felt, and transitory; that joy and pleasure, sadness and pain are fleeting; that life itself ultimately entails separation from those about whom we care the most and the loss of all that we cherish? After many years of study and personal growth, I have arrived at a paradoxical synthesis of sorts: Life is suffering, just as the Buddha taught, and so I seek a general transcendence of my attachments to things and relationships in this world. But then I remind myself, as my Jewish heritage affirms, that life is good and a blessing, so I also seek joyous engagement with all that life has to offer, and relationships above all. In a way, my effort at non-attachment may be a mild form of PTSD, but perfectly understandable given the experience of suffering that I have had. My re-embracing of life, on the other hand, is

---

5. If there is anything to the concept of "original sin," it is that what we experience as children, whether for good or bad, we tend to replicate and pass on as adults unless we really work at consciously choosing how we act.

6. For a wise analysis of life's losses, see Judith Viorst's *Necessary Losses*.

an expression of my hope for life renewed. It represents a conscious choice on my part because I know that when my grief was at its strongest the pull towards life's opposite was strong.

Live as If Today Were the Last Day of the Rest of Your Life

For Jews, death is not the annihilator of all meaning, rather it is an enhancer of meaning. Knowing that there is a time limit to all we do and love, we may better learn to cherish our time on earth. On Yom Kippur—a symbolic taste of death and the Day of Judgment, according to Jewish tradition—we ask forgiveness, first and foremost of ourselves, and then of our fellow human beings, and finally of God, for wasting time, for losing sight of that which is truly important in life. Yom Kippur and the preceding ten days are designed to help us get in touch with our mortality, to help get us back on track, to return to the Way, to try to do good better. What is required of us is that we strive to celebrate the blessings of our finitude by being faithful to our own potentialities and making the most of our lives.

One of the most common attributes of the traditional God concept is God's presumed ability to know the innermost secrets of our hearts. Consequently, a dying person would know that God would be looking at their deeds with an honesty we ourselves often lack, looking at the totality of who we are without the subjectivity that each of us has. Regardless of whether or not one believes in such a God, we might do well to take stock of our lives *as if* there were such a God, who sees through our transparent devices and self-serving deceptions, *as if* there were an actual Day of Judgment after death.

In my work with people who were dying of AIDS, we tried our best to help these individuals make peace with the course their lives has taken. This process, if one is fortunate, may include having the actual opportunity to reconcile with family and friends, with oneself, and with one's God. Reconciliation means recognizing that however good one has been in life, one always falls short of perfection. Acknowledging this fact and asking forgiveness for one's shortcomings is an essential part of this reconciliation process. The Rev. Gwen Beighle called this "dying a good death" and she herself later modeled just what she had so often talked about.

The nice part about dying a good death is that one need not wait until one is on one's deathbed to do it. Long ago, Rabbi Eliezar[7] told his disciples,

---

7. Rabbi Eliezar ben Hyrcanus, end of the first century and beginning of the second

"Repent one day before your death," to which his students then asked, "Does a person know on what day he will die; that he should know when to repent?" And to which the sage responded, "All the more that you should repent today lest you die tomorrow."[8]

In Hebrew, the word for "repentance" is *teshuvah*, but more literally it means "returning"—returning to walk along the path of God's instruction (Torah). The process of returning, of *teshuvah*, begins with a profound awareness of life and of death, with a sense of the preciousness of passing time. It continues with a reordering of your priorities and concludes with actual changes in your way of thinking and in your deeds.[9]

So when Rabbi Eliezar says "Repent one day before your death" he means that we should strive every day to live our lives with the same intensity as if we knew it was our last. Imagine how our lives would be if we chose to live each day as if it were the *last* day of the rest of our lives. We would be more focused on our relationships, more willing to forgive minor trespasses and perhaps even larger offenses too, more understanding of human foibles, more disposed to talk about things that really matter.

Years ago, good friends nearly lost their child. The girl hadn't been feeling well and was taken to the hospital the next day. That night her brain swelled up and she nearly died. Her parents were told to prepare for the worst. Incredibly, a doctor who specialized precisely in her condition happened to be on the floor that particular night, recognized her symptoms, and diagnosed her as having juvenile diabetes. After a five-hour procedure, her life was saved and now, though diabetic, she is doing fine and is now an adult. To this day, the coincidence in this story reminds me of the High Holy Day prayer in which God determines who shall live and who shall die; who by this, and who by that. It seemed *almost* to be a divine intervention that she survived.

This family, like any other, had its issues and problems. But when faced with the issue of life and death, what do all these ordinary things matter? They don't count even a whit. Business success or failure, squabbles

---

century of the Common Era.

8. *b. Shabbat* 153a.

9. This analysis is called *heshbon hanefesh*, an accounting of one's soul. Ideally it is done continually, but at least annually during the month of Ellul and Ten Days of Return between Rosh HaShannah and Yom Kippur, and finally in the days or hours before one's death. My friend Bruce Kochis pointed out to me that *teshuvah* need not be drastic; not a 180-degree turn but something less also is fine. He joked that 18 degrees is 10 percent of 180 degrees and that is a good amount of change for which to aim since "eighteen" in Hebrew is the numerical representation or equivalent for "life"—*chai* חי.

between spouses, siblings, and friends; all disappear and become meaningless. Because when confronting the merest possibility of death, you focus on the fragility and preciousness of life and your priorities get instantly rearranged for the better.

Another friend of mine blacked out while driving on a highway and came to with his car wrapped around a telephone pole. Medics said it was a miracle that he was alive—and indeed it was! This is how he understood what happened to him:

> One cannot help but ponder following an experience like this. I know members of my family would have been sad if I had died. I am immensely grateful for the realization that there were no unspoken conversations, secrets, old grudges, or unfinished business in any of my family relationships.
>
> I am grateful in the conviction that God is with me. God was with me in surviving that accident. God would have been present with me if I have been disabled in the accident. And God would have been present with me if I had not survived . . .
>
> This accident has been a profound reminder of the need for preparation throughout our lives. Embrace your spiritual path and all that gives meaning to life and prepares us for Eternal Life. We are not guaranteed days or years on Earth. Value relationships as if today is the last day with the ones we love.[10]

Any day can be a good day to die. There will always be more to do, more to accomplish, and more milestones to reach. There may be better or worse times to die in terms of its impact on your life plan or on loved ones, but it is always a good day to die—particularly if you are ready to depart with a "good name."

How does one acquire a "good name"? According to Jewish tradition, by the deeds we do and the way we behave. What matters in the end are the acts of kindness and the love that is shown to those whom we meet on life's path—family, friend, and stranger alike. It's what we hope to leave behind when we depart this life, secure in the knowledge that we have contributed positively in some small or large way towards improving life on this planet, so that when people recall you they will say, "May his/her memory be for a blessing," meaning that people will recall the good you strove to do in life and be motivated to act in a similar way. The epitaph of baseball great Jackie Robinson reads: "A life is important only for the impact it has on other lives." That is worth remembering and acting upon!

10. Christopher Szarke, Facebook post, December 2017.

One cannot deny the reality of grief. It just has to be lived through and slowly integrated into your being until hopefully you re-emerge somewhat healed and somewhat whole—and always somewhat broken. But life goes on and that is good.

Life *is* good; it is change and it is growth, and it will always find a way to persevere. I see it in plants cracking through cement or worming their way around boulders towards the light. I have seen it when vegetation and animal life return after cataclysmic disasters, whether natural or man-made. I have witnessed it in Holocaust survivors who chose to raise families and build new lives rather than give in to despair and suicide. And I have observed it in myself, a grieving man who happily has found love again but who nonetheless remains in the continual process of rebuilding his life. Grief is a forever kind of thing.[11]

Speculating about Dying and Death

Let me start by focusing on what is commonly called the "afterlife" or, as I prefer to call it, the "after-death." What happens after we die has always been a major source of religious speculation, and providing answers to this question has also been one of religion's chief tasks. Many faiths use the fear of death and the lure of an afterlife as a sort of spiritual club to dun adherents into proper moral behavior and correct belief in this world, promising all sorts of things to the worthy righteous after death. Pragmatically speaking, this is a positive outcome, but many religions also have linked the afterlife with a sense of presumptive judgment best left to God alone. Besides, how does one verify the benefit package?

Judaism is remarkably non-dogmatic regarding the after-death. Jews at one time or another have advocated a shadowy netherworld (*Sheol*); transmigration of the soul (*gilgul ha-nefesh*); an immortal soul that returns to God (*hayyei olam*); and, most normatively, belief in a personal physical resurrection (*tehiyyat ha-meitim*) after the coming of the Messiah and the Day of Judgment. But even with all this speculation, the focus of the faith has always been on the here-and-now because how one lives here determines what comes after, whatever the after-here is.

Perhaps this very diversity of ideas led me to realize, early on, that what was being taught went far beyond our ability to actually know. Since

---

11. Grief also can act like a terrorist because a grieving person never knows when or where it will strike.

whatever might exist after death *is* beyond our knowing, all ideas of the after-death *are* just ideas—images, dreams, wish fulfillment—requiring giant leaps of faith.[12] But what we really about it know is *bupkis* (Yiddish for "nothing")! Consequently, it was easy for me to let go of these traditional concepts—but finding a replacement, something that offers hope for some form of continuity, has been a more challenging endeavor.

At any rate, long ago I let go of the grave certainties of Jewish tradition in favor of the certainty of believing that this life is all there is. And for many years this sufficed. Now, however, where once I was a true believer in the finitude of life, today I am a skeptic. Two things worked together to change my mind on the subject of what happens to us after death.

The first was the realization that life is not only what it appears to us to be. Usually we think of ourselves as singular entities, just as we like to think of steel or wood as solids, or colors as colors, etc. But colors apparently are really the absences of light that have been absorbed, and what appears as solid is in fact a mass of swirling electrons. Similarly, what appears to us as a human being is actually a mass of various kinds of living cells and organisms, all working—one assumes unconsciously—more or less in harmony to allow us to function as we do. Were we to have the awareness, we would know that our bodies are alive, not just with us, but teeming with other life forms as well. There are dust mites and other critters on our outsides and micro-organisms in our insides, some of which are essential to our well-being, like those which live in our stomachs and aid with digestion, and others, like lice, which just enjoy our hospitality.

What appears and operates to you and me as you or me is in truth a universe of symbiotic systems. I sometimes wonder if I am an actual universe to those micro-organisms who share my body. I consider this and then wonder if our perception of things is as limited as theirs, both physically and spiritually. What exactly are we? What really is our existence? What constitutes reality? It is times like this that I believe that Dr. Seuss's *Horton Hears a Who* to be a most profound book of speculative metaphysics because it posits a entire unseen world existing on a piece of fluff.[13] The

---

12. Again, Richelle Harrell challenges my perception of things by pointing out that in Hindu and Buddhist traditions reincarnation is not only believed to occur but is actually experienced; witness the proofs required for each reincarnation of a Tibetan lama before he is accepted as such.

13. The book depicts a world within a world and reminds me of the Hindu stories illustrating *maya* (our illusory world) and the vastness of "real time" as opposed to "perceived time."

truth is that we know very little about anything—and that certainly includes what happens after death.

So when you think about life and death, existence and non-existence, think again. Things may not be as they seem. Think of all the billions of little lives you unknowingly maintain and, with them in mind, ask yourself again: What is reality? Life, big or small, apparent or imperceptible, is a profound mystery that invites our wonder and awe. Life is not always what it seems. That was my first awareness.

The second thing that helped change my thinking about death was my experience, over the years, of working with people dying of AIDS-related diseases and being able to observe dying and death firsthand, more so than I would have in a normal lifetime. I trace this change in perception to one of my first encounters with a dying person, who, fortunately for me, seemed to know what he was doing.

I had known "N," a Tibetan Buddhist monk, for a number of years through our work together on interfaith issues. I always had been impressed with his simplicity, his peace, his kind demeanor, and his thoughtfulness. I didn't know then that he had AIDS. Later, after I came to Multifaith Works, I invited him to join our interfaith pastoral care group. One day, he told us he had AIDS and was just recovering from a long battle against lymphoma. A week later he was in the hospital "just for a few days" because of PCP. A week later N was dead.

When I visited him in the hospital, it seemed to me that N just hovered in his bed. He had become so slight and so pale—ethereal really—that only the bedcovers restrained him from floating away. Every breath he took was an effort—I could hear the mucus rattle with his every inhalation—but he was peaceful. I began to look at him differently. He was no longer the person I knew as N. His body was there in bed, but *it* wasn't N. His body had become just a cage to his life force. (Dare I call it his soul?) Like a captive bird, it was just waiting to fly free once the cage door opened.

But that life force wasn't totally N either. The person I knew as N was both his life force and his body, and maybe something more besides. But now his life force was trapped in his failing body. I watched him breathe, his eyes closed, oblivious to the world around him. Then suddenly his eyes would open, and his body and soul would work in unison again. Suddenly my old friend was there once more, and he would smile at me and we'd talk. N was not in spiritual pain. His training as a Tibetan Buddhist was spent readying himself for the moment of death and liberation. He was at peace. He smiled at me, but needed nothing. He was waiting for the cage door to open. But I—I had seen the separation, and the image of the caged bird never left me.

Years later, while I was in Toronto to help see our mother through some heart surgery, this image of the caged bird came back to me. While recuperating, she was given some strong painkillers that made her temporarily delusional and occasionally paranoid. Her condition prompted me to reflect again on the interrelationship and connections between body, mind, and that mysterious other quality we call spirit.

Normally, when we look at a person, we see them as a totality: body and mind combined into one living being with a distinct personality—a human being. The components are usually inseparable. As Mum rambled on in her shadow world, she was forcing me—and I had to force myself—to disconnect the association I had maintained since birth about the unity of her mind and body.

Gradually, I began to better understand something about the human condition. Outwardly, my mother was physically the same person I knew and loved. But, under the influence of her medications, she had temporarily lost her mind. A person can lose a limb or organ without losing his/her identity. Although one may feel impaired in various ways, generally speaking, identity remains intact. But can a person lose a mind with the same impunity? I was forced to accept that although her body remained intact, her mind had gone elsewhere. But what did that mean? Was it either/or, or was it something more?

As I observed her, I came to realize that in addition to body and mind there *is* something more, something intangible, something that constitutes the sum of her life experiences: her personhood as she lived it, as I experienced it, and as others did too. It is more than personality or character, more than just the life force, certainly much more than presence of mind. Here on this bed lay a unique woman, one whom I knew but a little as her son. Even without her rational mind, somehow this person, this being, remained very present.

With my Buddhist friend, I first thought to compare the soul of a dying person to a bird trapped in a cage, awaiting the opportunity to fly free. That image remained and I called it to mind. Yes, my mother appeared near death, but on this occasion I also thought of the Hindu greeting *Namaste*. "I honor the God in you" is one of its many meanings. I realized that even without her mind my mother still existed for all that she had been and still was. Even when a mind goes, the person remains, present with us in every way but in mind. Something beautiful still exists and it is to this that we are called to say *Namaste*.

The ultimate question for me is this: When a body dies, the mind goes with it—we "disassemble," as my friend Gene Duvernoy puts it—so what happens to the formerly caged bird that is now set free? Where does that unique bit of animating energy go?

Over the years, I have seen a number of dying and dead people. The chasm between the dying and the dead is so vast that it embraces all the mysteries of the universe. The dying are alive; they breathe, they retain that life spark. The dead only resemble the living in form; in content the dead are something else.

All I can say about death and the after-death today is that I am convinced that the life force that exists in each of us, and indeed in every living thing—if not something more than the mere life force—must go somewhere. Our bodies are recycled, gone to nourish other living things, but energy does not disappear; it can only be transformed or transferred. Beyond this pale assertion, I cannot say more with any certainty. I *do* like to speculate that the particularity of our individual life forces—the totality of our life experiences—continues in some way too, but that is 100 percent conjecture and pure unadulterated hope.

A former coworker at Multifaith Works, Trudy James, believes that the "love energy," although immeasurable and unseen, that can be felt between lovers, even if separated by great distance, tells us that unexplainable connections exist in this world. Why can't it also exist between this life and the next? she wonders, citing as evidence the very real connection felt by many people with their deceased loved ones. Why not indeed? Who knows?

The work of Dr. Melvin Morse, who has documented and analyzed the near-death experiences of children, offers information that can lead to some interesting speculation precisely because it has a clinical foundation. According to his research, children who have nearly died and been revived share similar kinds of perceptions of their experience, regardless of their faiths or cultures.[14] So perhaps there is something of hope to which to cling deriving from these near-death experiences. At the very least, one may take comfort from the apparent fact that, even though we may never know what happens after death, it appears that once the pain associated with dying is

---

14. Melvin Morse, MD, studied near-death experiences in children for fifteen years and is the author of several popular books on the subject: *Closer to the Light, Transformed by the Light,* and *Parting Visions.*

done, the experience is not half bad. In fact, it even may be "pleasurable" in its serenity.

Beyond this, the most encouraging words about the after-death I have ever heard were told to me by my friend Wayne Lubin, who had suffered (or perhaps "had been blessed with") a near-death experience following a cerebral hemorrhage. Wayne told me that what he remembers is the great feeling of peacefulness that had embraced him, coupled with a sloughing off of daily concerns. To this day, he remains in touch with this feeling and, when asked, he says he is totally unafraid about death because of his experience. Unfortunately, he also said that the further in time he travels from his near-death experience, the more caught up in mundane anxieties he gets once again. (I suppose this proves that you can't take it with you—either from this world to the great beyond, or vice versa.)

There is a midrash that nourishes my thinking about death. In one famous speculation regarding what happens prior to birth, it was taught that souls dwell with God in Paradise, where they are privy to all the mysteries and secrets of the universe. There they stay until it is time for a baby to be born. Then, just as a soul is joined with a body prior to birth, an angel touches the fetus on the upper lip and all that soul's knowledge disappears. And that is why babies cry when they are born—they are lamenting all they no longer know—and it also explains why we are born with that indent on our upper lips.[15]

To me, this midrash is an equally great metaphor for the after-death because death may be a portal, just as birth is to this life. We honestly don't know. The main thing about death is this: Do not be afraid. Fear the pain of dying if you must—and thank God and doctor and nurse for the drugs. Make your peace with friends and family to the extent that you are able, but do not be afraid. The energy that marks each of us as unique and distinguishes us from that which is not alive endures. Is that cold comfort? Not for me; not right now.

15. *b. Niddah* 30b.

Chapter 11

Iyov Restored
My Personal Epilogue—Choosing Life

YHVH restored Iyov's fortunes ... YHVH blessed the latter years of Iyov's life ...
so Iyov died old and contented.
(Iyov 42:10, 12, 17)

THE BOOK OF IYOV has a fairytale ending. Iyov's fortunes are restored—
doubled in fact; he had new children and he died at a ripe old age. While my
family and I were going through our years of hell, people often compared
me to Iyov. Now that the cloud of suffering has moved on from our family,
I feel like Iyov restored. I have remarried and my new wife is a wonderful,
caring, and wise woman; I have two terrific daughters, three good sons-in-
law, four almost-grown grandchildren, and a new baby grandson. I've had
an interestingly diverse career, built up enough savings to retire comfortable (although I still waiting for God to double them), and I remain in
relatively good health. So what's to complain?

I wonder about Iyov's interior life post-restoration: Did he still grieve
for his dead children? Did he still shudder when he recalled all that had
befallen him? Did the harsh words of his former friends still bring tears
to his eyes? I know that I remain forever haunted by the trauma of what I
endured. Even my happiest moments are grayed with a little grief. There is
no forgetting, only a patching over the past with new life experiences. I live

restored and content, but wounded nonetheless. And I continually think about what it all means to me.

In the course of this book, I have debunked (at least to my own satisfaction) many of the traditional explanations for suffering and come to the conclusion that what happens in life is largely a matter of chance. God does not appear to play an active role either in the events of our personal lives or in history, and responding to injustice and suffering, whether natural or man-made, is a human task, not God's. As a consequence of this belief, I rejected the traditional concept of prayer, which is based on asking for God's intercession, and came to focus on expressing gratitude, being present in the moment, and seeking self-transformation as alternate forms of prayer. I deconstructed the traditional God-concept of the Abrahamic faiths and built something new based on the ineffable experience of the divine mystery. As a consequence of this belief, I came to see revelation as a human response to that mystery, one that is global in its expression and accessible to everyone (although not necessarily on the same level). Now I will try to put all that I have experienced, and all that I have thought, together in a meaningful way based on the values I have come to cherish. In this chapter, I will explore how best to live, both as individual human beings and collectively, as one human family together with all other living creatures on this planet.

I   THE CHOICE BEFORE EACH OF US

In the book of *Dvarim/Deuteronomy*, Moshe lays before the children of Yisrael—and by extension, all of us—a loaded choice of momentous proportions: God offers us "life" or "death"; "blessing" or "curse"; "good" or "bad."[1] God, we are told, wants us to choose the good—life and blessing, not death and curse—and invites us to follow the commandments, or face the consequences. (*This* is a choice?!)

In all the Abrahamic faiths, the traditional God certainly is not above using fear and threats to manipulate humanity into doing good. However, we can choose "life" and "blessing" without fear simply because it makes sense to do so. We can think differently. Marianne Williamson, in her book *A Return to Love*, suggests that we have internalized senses of fear and love the consequences of which appear as "curses" and "blessings" in our world.

---

1. Dvar/Deut 30:15, 19. The latter pair is often translated as "prosperity" and "adversity."

She identifies fear as "our shared lovelessness" and sees its expression in a host of evils including selfishness, greed, addiction, abuse, and war.[2] Love, on the other hand, is expressed and experienced as lovingkindness, mercifulness, compassion, joyfulness, and so on. We can choose, with every action, whether to "extend love" or "extend fear"—the blessing and the curse.[3]

There are, of course, constraints on our free will. It is shaped by factors such as heredity, environment, and social context. But, even given these constraints, we all still choose to do actions that are either constructive or destructive, each with far-reaching consequences. There is no way to measure the full or ultimate impact of our deeds and behavior because the choices we make are transformative both for their impact on ourselves and on others. It is important, therefore, to appreciate and acknowledge even the smallest actions—like acting kindly or speaking courteously—because even these simple gestures build the potential for more good will and right action. When we choose to take positive, constructive actions in our own lives and in the lives of others, we are focusing our energies on the life-affirming blessings that come from choosing to do good. In the Jewish tradition, we have a saying: "One *mitzva* [commandment or good deed] leads to another"—good deeds work like infinite ripples in a pond, spreading outwards, influencing others. (Bad deeds also work in the same way.) We recreate potentiality, or new possibilities, with every act we do, whether good or bad, because our every action ripples out with infinite consequences.

Oftentimes life is harsh. One image I have of the human experience is that in this sometimes cold and dangerous world of ours, this world of random chaos and violence, caring people must stand together like a herd of musk oxen, maintaining warmth and protection for one another by standing shoulder to shoulder in a circle, the more vulnerable ones on the

---

2. Williamson, *Return to Love*, xxi–xxii; 17–26.

3. It is easy to see a divine presence in good deeds and, in truth, I believe YHVH is *more* present there than in anything else. But not all we do is good. What of less noble deeds? Some deeds have more of a divine presence, others less; all to some degree are tainted to soured to spoiled with selfishness and self-deception. The quality of our deeds depends on two factors: the action itself and its motivation or intention. Actions speak for themselves, but the impetus for action is known only to doer (who may be self-deceiving) and, as it were, to God.

I believe there is no such thing as a wholly evil person because even the worst person imaginable seems to have had at least a few good qualities. Demonizing bad people minimizes the problem—the real horror is the ordinariness of people who do evil and the evil doings of ordinary people.

inside and many pairs of horns facing outward. Life's crises are never easy, but by treating one another with lovingkindness and empathy—by standing together like a herd of yakking musk oxen—we can help support one another through almost everything. God may not be invoked to assist from on high—and even if invoked, it is highly unlikely God will intervene—but YHVH will somehow be present in the lovingkindness shown, in the solidarity demonstrated, and in the love shared. It is clear that in helping one another it matters little what religion you have or even whether you have a religion at all. What counts is that we choose to be engaged and that *we* act.

Love means standing together, hoping together, building together. Love builds even when life's experiences may destroy. Through love, we can defy, delay, and, for a time, even reverse this process of entropy. As Elie Wiesel taught through the characters in so many of his novels, we need to learn to dance and sing in defiance of whatever life throws our way. We need to capture whatever joy happens to exist, be grateful for it, magnify it, and use it to conquer the looming despair that so often accompanies the random misfortunes of illness, suffering, and death. This defiant joy, this hope against hope, and the grateful sharing of little things makes life more bearable, because the suffering is tempered, counterbalanced, and sometimes even displaced by the positive feelings being shared.[4]

Simply put, our task is to learn how to show love to one another. Love is what makes of life a blessing.

---

4. This same principle can be applied to social issues. My friend Julie Pfau observed the following:

> during study of shemot, i was confronted with a passage that once would have inspired anger in me—the statement that god heard the cries of the hebrews and remembered the covenant . . . i suggested that when people cry out, other people are forced to hear the cries—the cries break through the walls of others and the result can be a new openness to the idea that something needs to be done to end that pain. in this state of openness to the reality and horror of oppression, they can grow leaders who will change that condition. another congregant then picked up from there and brought in what i think will be an important new dimension to my theology—sometimes a critical mass is needed before significant growth can happen. there must be enough people who are open, because if there aren't enough people then the growth might not be able to break through . . .

II   WHAT IS REQUIRED OF US

And how do we practice love? According to Jewish teaching, although we have free will to choose how we act, God, as it were, encourages us along the right path by giving us the commandments, all centering around the idea that we should emulate God in our behavior—as in "Be holy, for I, YHVH your God, am holy."[5] In a general way, when we are told to emulate God in holiness, we are to act as God ideally is supposed to act—at least when he's on his best biblical behavior. From a Jewish theological perspective, one learns loving behavior from God, then we use these principles ever more specifically as we strive apply them in the course of everyday life.[6]

And what constitutes the specifics of this model behavior? In God's purported self-disclosure to Moshe on Mt. Sinai, God uses these words of self-characterization: "YHVH, YHVH [the LORD, the LORD], a God merciful and gracious, slow to anger, abounding in lovingkindness and faithfulness, extending lovingkindness to the thousandth generation, forgiving iniquity, transgression, and sin."[7] Known as the Thirteen Attributes of Mercy, this phrase serves as the basis for divine forgiveness in Judaism and thus, following Moshe's own use of it in a time of crisis,[8] Jews quote these words back to God as a divine reminder in Jewish penitential services, most significantly on Yom Kippur (the Day of Atonement) and when the Torah is read.

What is remarkable, however, is that the rabbinic authors of the liturgy purposefully chose to ignore everything else God had to say about himself

5. Vay/Lev 19:2. The chapter from which this verse is taken, called the Holiness Code, contains many examples about what in Judaism it means to be holy and to emulate God.

6. Much of Jewish tradition has focused on the here-and-now because of its emphasis on *mitzvot* and there is also a school of thought, called *musar* or *mussar*, which focuses primarily on improving one's character and behavior. Of late, *musar* has been enjoying a revival in the American Jewish world. Several books worth reading are: Morinis, *Everyday Holiness* and *Climbing Jacob's Ladder*; Stone, *Responsible Life*; and Winkler and Elior, *Place Where You Are Standing Is Holy*.

7. Shem/Exod 34:6–7. This is as close as Torah comes to describing/limiting God and it is used frequently in the Tanakh: Bam/Num 14:18–19; Yoel/Joel 2:13; Yonah/Jonah 4:2; Mich/Mic 7:18; Teh/Pss 86:15; 103:8; 145:8; Neh 9:17, 31; 2 Div/Chr 30:9. Ultimately, what is shown to Moshe on Sinai is little different in content than what he had been told at the start of his career. Then he was told, "I am who/what I am"; now he is told, "I will be gracious to whom I am gracious." Poor Moshe! In both cases, the circular answer Moshe receives shows that YHVH will not be limited; that, although YHVH's qualities may be tasted, YHVH is ultimately unknowable.

8. Bam/Num 14:17–19.

in that same verse. It continues: "yet he does not remit all punishment, but visits the iniquity of parents upon children and children's children, upon the third and fourth generations." Talk about *chutzpah*! How could the rabbis of old so arbitrarily "censor" God? I think they did so to make a point. What the people needed from their God was lovingkindness and forgiveness, not more judgmental behavior and punishment. So the rabbis simply amended God's self-description! In the context of their prayers for forgiveness, the rabbis were attempting to focus the people's attention on God's loving qualities and, as it were, to remind God of them as well because this is God at his very best!

It is likewise all too easy for us to be judgmental and unforgiving and punitive; the challenge for us—as apparently for God—resides in being loving and understanding. I believe that the rabbis wanted us to strive for those divine qualities we often lack—not the ones that unfortunately come so naturally to so many of us. *It is no sin to err on the side of compassion*; this is a principle that applies just as surely to relations between human beings and nations as it does to God's relationship with us. It is precisely when we act compassionately and lovingly that we are fulfilling the commandment "to be holy like God is holy."

But what does "being holy" or "showing lovingkindness" entail? Let me again use my Jewish particularity as a point of departure to elaborate. Jews would want to know specifics about what this means, and how to do it, how often, and so forth. Viewing the world through covenantal lenses, the rabbis in the early centuries of the Common Era taught that humanity in general, and the Jewish people in particular, are partners with God in the process of redemption[9] and believed that all human beings are obligated to observe God's commandments. Although everyone has commandments, observing the commandments is the specific Jewish path to the divine, which is why there are more commandments for Jews as a result of their (self-perceived) unique covenant with God and only seven universal ones for all the other children of Noach (Noah). This is the so-called Noahide

---

9. Consider the following midrash (*Pesikta Rabbati* 31): "My Torah is in your hands but the End (of Days) is in My hands. We need each other. Just as you need Me to bring the End, so too I need you to observe My Torah . . ." And in another famous midrash, *Jerusalem Talmud* Hagigah 1:7, God, as it were, declares that the commandments are so important that he would prefer the people forsake him than forget to observe the commandments!

Covenant.[10] Practicing the commandments is how, according to Jewish tradition, we love God and our fellow human beings both.[11]

But it doesn't end there. The Talmud records a discussion by several rabbis in which they have Israel's prophets reducing the number of commandments down to their essentials, which were as few as one, depending on which prophet was cited.[12] It is no coincidence that Jesus, as a Jewish teacher of the first century, also formulated his own summary of the commandments by quoting, "You shall love the Lord your God with all your heart, and with all your soul, and with all your might" . . . "You shall love your neighbor as yourself."[13] Of these he taught: "On these two commandments depend all the law and the prophets" and "There is no commandment greater than these."[14]

In a similar fashion, a midrash records a "debate" between rabbis of different generations about the greatest principle in the Torah. Rabbi Akiva said, "'You shall love your neighbor as yourself'—that is the greatest principle in the Torah"; but Shimon ben Azzai said, "The sentence 'This is

10. The seven Noahide laws generally are enumerated as: do not practice idolatry; do not blaspheme; do not murder; do not engage in illicit sexual relations; do not steal; do not eat parts of a live animal; and establish courts of law.

11. Since the commandments were understood to be the very word of God (as interpreted and modified by the prophets, sages, and rabbis), the more scrupulously observed the better. (Judaism is a great religion for obsessive people.) Under the traditional conception of God, the motivation to follow God's will derived from a mixture of love, fear, and awe. To this, the rabbis added a reward or punishment system focused on the World to Come, which was both an inducement to better behavior and also a way of dealing with the obvious inequities and injustices of this world.

My teacher, the late Arthur Lagawier, noted that in Hebrew the Ten Utterances (the Ten Commandments) are written in the future tense, as though to say, "If you understand the rationale behind these words (i.e., what is required of us as mature human beings), then 'you will honor' and 'you will not murder' etc." To use his analogy: a teenager may need the threat of punishment to obey the speed limit, but a mature adult knows the dangers involved in speeding and so will follow the law of his own volition and not from fear of being caught and fined, or injured.

12. *b. Makkot* 23b–24a. Daveed/David, it was said, summed up the commandments in ten principles; the prophet Yeshayahu/Isaiah brought the number down to six; Michah/Micah then reduced them to three; whereupon Yeshayahu/Isaiah returned and reduced them to two; and finally Habakkuk summed them up with one principle: "the righteous one shall live by [or through] his faith." The respective proof texts cited are: Teh/Ps 15; Yesh/Isa 33:15–16; Mich/Mic 6:8; Yesh/Isa 56:1; and Hav/Hab 2:4.

13. Dvar/Deut 6:5 and Vay/Lev 19:18, respectively.

14. Matthew 22:36–40 and Mark 12:29–31, respectively.

the book of the generations of man . . . '[15] is even greater than the other," because it points to the unity of humankind being created in the image of the divine. Rabbi Tanhuma, a third participant, taught that one should *not* interpret "Love your neighbor as yourself" to mean that if you despise yourself you may also treat your neighbor similarly. Just the opposite: he is and will always be a being made in the image of God.[16] For this same reason, my teacher, the late Arthur Lagawier, translated the verse as "Love your neighbor. S/he is like you."[17] Translating it this way, he thought, stressed the point that all human beings are endowed with equal, inalienable worth and should be treated accordingly.

For me, the question is best framed thusly: Do the commandments, *however observed*, add holiness to the life of the individual and enhance a person's relationships with other human beings and also with God? *If* they impart value and direction to everyday life, *if* they assist in dealing with life's transitions, *if* they help awaken a sense of wonder to the mystery of Creation and to YHVH's presence in it, *if* they nurture a feeling of profound gratitude, and *if* they contribute to improving the world—*then* they are as important and as valid *as if* they had come directly from the mouth of God.

In the Jewish tradition, the path to holiness resides in the practices of daily life, and in our relationships in particular. The prophet Hosheiya (Hosea) has God declare: "I will espouse you with righteousness [*tsedek*] and justice [*mishpat*], and with lovingkindness [*hesed*], and compassion [*rachamim*], and I will espouse you with faithfulness [*emunah*]"[18]—and as the divine-human relationship goes, so too should human-to-human relationships if we are to emulate God. These values—righteousness, justice, lovingkindness, mercy, and faithfulness—are the ways we express love in the world. Although all are intertwined, and without denigrating any one of them, I think that *hesed* חסד is most important for the topic at hand. *Hesed* is often translated as "steadfast love," but I prefer to translate it as "lovingkindness." *Hesed* has within itself overtones and hints of mercy, compassion, favor, faithfulness, goodness, piety, benevolence, righteousness, and graciousness.

From *hesed* come *gemilut hasadim*, acts of lovingkindness. The rabbis taught (perhaps playfully) that God personally performed various deeds of

15. Ber/Gen 5:1

16. *Sifra* 89b and also *Bereisheet Rabbah* 24:7.

17. The Hebrew word *kamocha* is usually translated "as yourself" but he chose to translate it also correctly as "s/he is like you."

18. Hosh/Hos 2:21–22.

lovingkindness for us to emulate: God clothed the naked (Ahdam/Adam and Hava/Eve), visited the infirm (Avraham, after his circumcision), and buried the dead (Moshe), among other things.[19] Again, God's purported behavior becomes the model for us to emulate. So important is the practice of lovingkindness that one sage, Shimon the Just, taught that the world is sustained by three things: (the study of) Torah, worship, and deeds of lovingkindness.[20] A later sage, Rav Huna, taught that a person who studied Torah but did no deeds of lovingkindness was like one who had no God.[21] *Hesed* is the crucial Jewish principle for living a holy and good life.

The Mishnah teaches that there is no limit to the performance of deeds of lovingkindness[22] and that—along with the commandments of honoring one's parents, making peace between people, and studying Torah—they benefit a person in this world while (as it were) accruing merit in the World to Come (which may be just another way of stating the ripple effect). Deeds of lovingkindness are the quintessential, demonstrable acts of Jewish piety and the desire to be godly or holy.

One of my rabbinic heroes is the sage Hillel, who lived from about 60 BCE to 10 CE. He is best remembered for casting the Jewish version of the Golden Rule—"What is hateful to you, do not do to your fellow human being. That is the whole Torah, the rest is commentary. Now go and study."[23]—but he also taught a great deal about acting with *hesed*. He transformed Moshe's brother, Aharon, into the model for *hesed*, as for example in this saying: "Be of the disciples of Aharon, loving peace and pursuing peace, loving living creatures and bringing them close to the Torah."[24] Along with the Golden Rule, Hillel also taught the importance of empathy before judging another;[25] nonetheless, he also knew that acting with lovingkindness sometimes meant one had to behave courageously: "In a place where no one is acting as a human being should [literally, 'where there are no men'], strive to be a decent human being."[26] Hillel believed that by personally acting with *hesed*, people would be drawn to seek the source of his behavior and end up learning Torah; that learning Torah in turn would lead to a

19. *b. Sotah* 14a.

20. *Pirkei Avot* 1:2.

21. *b. Avodah Zarah* 17b.

22. *m. Pe'ah* 1:1.

23. *b. Shabbat* 31a.

24. *Pirkei Avot* 1:12.

25. *Pirkei Avot* 2:5.

26. *Pirkei Avot* 2:6.

profound spiritual awareness and acts of lovingkindness; and this in turn would lead to more peace, harmony, and understanding in the world.[27]

There are so many opportunities in daily life to practice *hesed*, but none provides as frequent an opportunity as speech. Speech is an essential building block to loving behavior and this is most apparent when speaking appropriately is a challenge. The ancient rabbis offered guidance on how to communicate well. They believed that the world would be better on a daily basis if straight talk and honest, loving communication were used, so they eulogized the process of giving and taking criticism.[28] Christianity shares this concern too—witness Jesus' words in Matthew 18:15–22, which is the Christian version of the rabbinic process of offering and receiving criticism.[29] To borrow from the Buddhist Eightfold Path: "right thought" and "right intention" lead to "right speech" and ultimately to "right action." Communication and action are integrally connected because how we interact is based on how we communicate and vice versa. Sometimes we give in to fears and don't speak or behave in this ideal way, but by accepting and forgiving (and having God forgive) our failures and then making positive changes, we can self-correct and redirect our lives back onto the right path.

Because doing *hesed* has a positive ripple effect, we can observe the good that often results. Through caring relationships, we nurture those qualities in us that motivated our good deeds in the first place and this, in turn, encourages us to continue on the path of *hesed*. Ideally it will also inspire the recipient of *hesed* to act similarly to another person too, paying that initial good deed forward.[30]

I like to think that YHVH is present in both the deed and the relationship. I have witnessed this positive, transformational Presence manifested in people coming together to help other people living with AIDS and other life-threatening diseases; I have seen it in how family and friends rallied to

27. *Pirkei Avot* 2:8. An excellent introduction to Hillel is Buxbaum, *Life and Teachings of Hillel*. See also Glatzer, *Hillel the Elder*.

28. A wonderful and accessible resource for learning more about the Jewish way of effective communication and other basic Jewish values is Klagsbrun, *Voices of Wisdom*.

29. My colleague the Rev. Anthony Robinson, a minister of the United Church of Christ variety, wrote a wonderful column titled "Articles of Faith" in the now-defunct *Seattle Post-Intelligencer* regarding these verses in *Matthew*, taking pains to show that, like Jesus, to be a Christian doesn't mean being nice to everyone all the time.

30. See, for example, "Pay It Forward" in *Psychology Today*, July 18, 2006, and Susan Skog, "The Give-Back Solution: Create a Better World with Your Time, Talents and Travel (Whether You Have $10 or $10,000)" and other materials on the website PersonalSafetyNets.com.

our side when my wife had ovarian cancer; and I have observed it in the self-less actions of friends and total strangers from all over the world striving to find a bone marrow match for our daughter when she had leukemia. I also see it when I read or hear about people reaching out to help other people, total strangers, after natural or man-made disasters.

Whether we are responding to the needs of a loved one or an un-known individual or an entire people, there are few things we do that are as noble as caring for other people. But, for many of us, it is easier to care for people from afar than it is to do so personally. Many people seem to fear coming in contact with people who are sick and those in mourning, let alone actually wading into a humanitarian crisis. Experiences like these make most of us anxious and uncomfortable, myself included. Perhaps it is instinctive, perhaps it is superstitious; I don't know. Even with training, it is emotionally and spiritually challenging to be present in such settings. In situations like these, it is always important to remember that the people who are suffering are at the center of the crisis, not us; that they need us to be there, to stand with them, to listen to them, to celebrate the little joys, and to surround them with compassion.[31]

My mentor at Multifaith Works, the late Rev. Gwen Beighle, called this sort of activity a "ministry of presence" and saw its task as, not to console with theology or prayer, but simply to be present with the person one was attending. A nurse's practical yet compassionate care, a doctor's humane concern, a relative's hug or friend's gentle touch—all potentially have great impact because they can break through the wall of isolation that suffering builds. The same holds true if we get involved in the humanitarian issues of our day. When we dare to act with lovingkindness, we are making a real difference because God has no other hands than ours with which to care for and comfort people in need.[32] And when we assist other people, when we act with lovingkindness, when we show love to one another, we are helping to build up, as it were, YHVH's positive presence in the world.

---

31. Some excellent, helpful books for these situations are: Bartlow, *Medical Care of the Soul*; Callanan and Kelley, *Final Gifts*; Gibson and Pigott, *Personal Safety Nets*; and Larson, *Helper's Journey*.

32. The phrase belongs to German theologian Dorothee Soelle (1929–2003). She has observed: "God has no other hands than ours. If the sick are to be healed, it is our hands that will heal them. If the lonely and the frightened are to be comforted, it is our embrace, not God's, that will comfort them."

III MY LEAP OF FAITH:
WHAT WE DO ALSO MATTERS TO YHVH

My leap of faith, therefore, is to affirm that what we do, how we act, some-how matters to YHVH; not in the personal way that traditional religions posit our behavior to be tallied by a father/judge God, but in some way nonetheless, because everything we do has far-reaching effects. Life is like YHVH; it is what it is—I don't see any master plan in operation, nor does YHVH appear to intervene in the world, nor is everything all rosy. But when I really listen to my gut, then I hold a fluttering hopeful sensation that YHVH may somehow participate in what happens here and that is for the better.

I do not believe this is mere wishful thinking. First of all, I know that YHVH is capable of being experienced. *I know this because I have experienced it.* From that singular experience I have maintained the sensation that I am/we are organically—spiritually, if you will—part of a greater Whole. Second, an equally important part of my formative spiritual experience was a profound sense of the "goodness" of Creation. Not that everything is good—because clearly it is not—but Creation is good in the sense of life tending toward the positive and the fulfillment of its potential, and the beauty that exists in that process. When I remind myself that I have felt YHVH in this way, then I feel that life gains in significance because of this Presence. Life is good; it is a blessing. Put more traditionally, this is what God wants for us.

I wish I could also assert that, somehow and in some way, our con-structive deeds actually enhance YHVH's presence in our world and that our negative actions somehow actually diminish YHVH's presence as well, but I cannot go quite this far. What I can say for certain is that *our sense* of YHVH's presence in the world is affected by how we act. Consider the period between the two world wars. It is not a stretch to consider that the traumas of World War I and the fear brought on by the Great Depression led to the brutality of fascism, Nazism and Stalinism, and that the Allies' initial failure to stand up to these cultures of fear contributed to the greatest slaughter in human history, some sixty million casualties all told. Human-ity's sense of basic goodness and its ability to act decently was incrementally weakened by ripples of increasingly negative behavior. In Martin Buber's phrase: It was a time of the "eclipse of God," when the good that exists in our society was obscured, temporarily, by the bad, and with it our sense of God's presence here. Conversely, when people respond to the needs of unknown others in times of natural disasters like the tsunami in Southeast Asia or an earthquake in Turkey, China, Haiti or Nepal, or both in Japan, or when people respond appropriately to political atrocities such as the ethnic cleansing in Bosnia, or 9/11 in America, or the genocide in Darfur, then I feel *as though* God's presence is being built up and that, in turn, we are strengthened and encouraged by that activity. Regardless of what happens on God's end, people are strengthened and encouraged by the positive actions of other people. One might even say that this is how God acts in history.

True it is that God, as the Source of All, is the origin of both good and evil. Equally true it is that we are ultimately responsible for our own actions. But there is more to it than this. I like to imagine that there is a scale balancing good and evil in this world and that human behavior affects this balance. If good and evil are more or less in balance, then goodness flows into the world (because I like to think that Creation tilts that way); but when human actions tilt to the side of evil, then imbalance results and bad incidences increase. And if more people do good—who knows?—it might herald the proverbial coming of the Messiah, or at least a messianic age (for a while).

How do we get there? By increasing our trust in one another. In Hebrew, the word for "trust" (*emunah*) is complexly nuanced because it is related to "truth" and "belief," to "nursing", and to being "supportive," "reliable," and "faithful." All derive from a common root, a-m-n אמן. (We also get the word "amen" from this root.) Since they are all interrelated, then there is another leap of faith that I take—that we all might take—and that is to dare to trust ourselves and one another to be reliable and compassionate—even if this runs counter to historical or personal experience. Trust is a psychological process, a spiritually transformative experience, and a personal commitment to our individual and collective potential to build a growing force for good in the world. To take this leap of faith and to truly trust other human beings is to begin the process of redemption because it nurtures a sense of hope. For some people, this long jump goes even further, extending to the belief—or having faith—that God actively cares for us as individuals, for humanity and all Creation. Bravo to those who can take this extra leap—but, as for myself, my head informs me that trust in God and humanity is unwarranted while my heart implores me both to trust and to be trustworthy nonetheless. So leap I must, to vault over my fears and dare to trust.

IV THE CHALLENGES FACING US TODAY

There is a midrash that has made it into the popular consciousness. The story is told of several men who were out in a boat together. One man started boring a hole under his seat. Alarmed, the other men began to complain vociferously, only to be met with the rebuke, "What concern is it to you? I am making the hole under my seat, not yours!"[33]

Today, most people know that drilling beneath one seat can sink the entire ship—although there are still some myopic individuals and nations that think and act otherwise. Nowadays, more than ever before, thanks to modern technology, we human beings are developing a consciousness of our unitary world and shared state of existence. A millennium ago, people on the various continents lived mostly in isolation from one another. At best, they had only minimal knowledge of each other's existence. When years began to be counted, pagans, Jews, Christians, Muslims, and the peoples of India, China, and everywhere else each counted time in their own way.

To be sure, Jews still count the years distinctively, as do Christians, Muslims, and others too, but the truth is that we also really do share a "Common Era." That we now count the years the same way is an indicator that we really have begun to think as one world. Not only this: In our day, we can watch live on various media events as they happen across the globe! In our day, we know that climate change affects us all, regardless of the degree to which we contribute to it. No longer can we pretend that any of us can operate in isolation—what we do here, and the choices we make, has an impact everywhere else. Increasingly we perceive that we—and our world—are one organic whole and interdependent. (You don't have to take my word for it. Just consider the pictures of the earth as photographed by astronauts en route to the moon. From that vantage point, our national and international squabbles, our religious disputes, all vanish into the thin swirling bubble of life that defines our little blue planet.)

The rabbis taught that humanity was created from a single pair so that no one could claim a superior lineage to anyone else.[34] Stripped of

33. *Vayikra Rabbah* 4:6.
34. *b. Sanhedrin* 38a.

all ephemera and external trappings, we are but endless variations of our prototypical mythic parents, coping with the same hopes and fears, dreams and nightmares, as have all people down through the ages. Life isn't any more complicated than this. We are the same; we are one and we are part of the divine Oneness. We are all bound together and interdependent.

I think that we are nearing a time when there will occur a shift in perception and attitude as great as that which occurred in the first centuries of the Common Era, a time of great political and cultural interaction—which led to the births of Rabbinic Judaism, Christianity, and Islam. Although the period was awash in conflict as various empires clashed and vied for power, nonetheless, as a result, theological/ philosophical ideas flowed freely: from the Mediterranean basin to the Middle East to Central Asia and beyond— and back again. It was a time when people sought, envisioned, and adopted God-concepts, ideas, and ways of worship far different than the ones that had worked for centuries prior.[35]

We may be approaching the cusp of a similar major change in our theologies today. As we gradually become a global civilization, we are ever so slowly replacing the anthropomorphic, personal, intercessory, and supernatural God of our traditions with God-concepts that are based on our newer understandings of our place in the universe, on modern cosmology, on the apparent laws of nature, and on mutual respect for our various faith traditions.[36] But this shift is occurring with great conflict—witness the rise of Jewish, Christian, Islamic, and even Hindu extremism as people react fearfully to these impending changes.

In order to proceed along the path to this sense of global, interconnected awareness—if it is to occur at all—I think that we need to recognize that all religions have healthy and unhealthy spiritual aspects, depending ultimately on whether they build on fear or love. A healthy spirituality, it

35. See for example, Armstrong, *Great Transformation*, on an earlier period of spiritual growth.

36. Wayne Teasdale in *The Mystic Heart* details this emerging consciousness, which he calls the Interspiritual Age, and believes it will focus on our essential interdependence with one another, with other species, with our planet.

The late Rabbi Zalman Schachter-Shalomi, or Reb Zalman as he preferred to be called, said that worldview-shattering events, such as Auschwitz or Hiroshima, necessitate a paradigm shift because they rendered many aspects of traditional Jewish theology irrelevant. At the same time, he felt they also had the transformative power to launch a new era of human civilization, one in which all human beings would reach out toward one another rather than continuing to live in fear and mistrust. See Singer, ed., *Paradigm Shift*.

seems to me, should be a positive force both in one's own life and in the lives of others, even as it connects one with the One. Healthy spirituality celebrates human creativity and individual uniqueness even while linking us to our particular religious and cultural roots. A healthy spirituality does not fear "the other"; it allows each person and faith a room of its own to develop in peace; it cannot be built on the backs of other people.

An unhealthy spirituality leads to fear-based, judgmental religious ideas and ideologies that drive people to the dark side of life and result in much of the human suffering. The recent spate of books detailing religion's many failures and flaws are basically correct in their analysis and should be heeded because our religions have been and still are forces for violence and oppression in many forms and in many places.[37]

But these books tell only a portion of the story. Our religions can play an important and positive role in our evolving human consciousness if, instead of focusing on what divides one religion from another and one people from another, we choose to focus on those things that our faiths share—ways to sanctify life's stages, values by which to live, ways to improve the world in which we live, and insights into that which lies beyond our finitude. As human beings, we are all dealing with the same experiences, concerns, and needs. And, with the humility that is becoming of limited creatures, mere mortals, it might be good to acknowledge how little we truly know of the divine or anything else for that matter. The key is to foster healthy spirituality, both individually and collectively, and to bravely and trustingly reach out to those of different backgrounds who are doing likewise.

The challenge for those of us who are trying to build cross-cultural and interfaith relations is that we are attempting to redirect a behavioral pattern that is almost instinctive—the tendency for people to associate only with their own kind. But the truth is that sometimes you may have more in common with a person of a different faith or background with whom you share a similar perspective than with someone from your own faith who does not share your outlook on life or who approaches others from a closed and hostile belief system. We will have to reverse centuries of negative religious energy and the sad human impulse to seek conformity in belief in

37. See Dawkins, *God Delusion*; Harris, *End of Faith*; Hitchens, *God Is Not Great*; and Lobdell, *Losing My Religion*. Coming from the opposite end, but offering an equally devastating critique of religion's failings—and maybe even more compelling because he is a deeply religious man—is Jonathan Sacks's *Not in God's Name*.

order to succeed in forging a new path.[38] But I believe with all my heart that it is possible.

In our world today it often seems as though the forces of fear-fed fundamentalism of various faiths (including ideologues of any stripe) are winning and driving all the rest of us, willy-nilly, into mutually exclusive camps. But we have one thing going for us that these people don't. Though not zealous or predisposed to violence in word or deed, we can choose to reach out to one another and form coalitions of compassion and cooperation where they cannot, because as much as these fundamentalists loathe our kind, they hate one another even more. There can be strength in the unity of our diversity.[39]

Humanity is one. And because we are one, we are challenged to work together, to put our shared spiritual/religious values into practice to help one another live and flourish, to sustain all living creatures, and to preserve our planet. This is what the future demands of us if humanity is to survive. It is, I think, what has always been asked of us. It is inspiring to see how in response to a crisis or catastrophe we can begin to function as a human family overnight, regardless of race, religion, or nationality. We can also see it in good times, like the opening of the Olympic Games, when athletes of all nations parade together in the opening ceremony. In times like these, good or bad, we demonstrate that we know, in our heart of hearts, that we are one. And it is just at times like these—when we see the good that we are capable of doing—that we get glimpses of who we truly are and could yet be.

I do not despair at the magnitude of the task before us. In the little more than one hundred years since the first World Parliament of Religions was held in Chicago, the modern interfaith movement has firmly taken root and spread among like-minded individuals around the world. After centuries of religious intolerance and bloodshed, humanity may have begun to embark on a new course. We have come a long way in just over one hundred years—and that is cause for hope.

---

38. My friends Rabbi Ted Falcon, Imam Jamal Rahman, and Pastor Don Mackenzie are trailblazers in this regard. See their books *Getting to the Heart of Interfaith* and *Religion Gone Astray*.

39. Like the Charter for Compassion movement, founded by Karen Armstrong: charterforcompassion.org.

V   LIVE YOUR VERSION OF THE GOLDEN RULE

Living love is what I think every faith ideally is all about. For example, at Multifaith Works I saw many people acting on the most noble beliefs and values of their respective faiths. Christians, Jews, Unitarians, Buddhists, New Thought, Latter Day Saints, New Age, Muslims, Baha'is, Wiccans, Hindus, humanists—you name it—all coming together to help people with AIDS in need of housing, care, and emotional and spiritual support. The motivating factors were different but the resultant behavior was identical!

This same principle of noble cooperation can apply to almost every issue confronting humanity today, from environmental degradation to alleviating poverty and disease to resolving conflicts. The work transcends every faith tradition and every culture; it belongs to all of us yet exclusively to none of us.

I believe that the concept of lovingkindness is universal; it is only articulated differently. What in the Jewish tradition is called *hesed* is analogous to the concepts of *agape* and *caritas* in Christianity, to *rakhma* in Islam, to *karuna* in Buddhism, to *ren* and *de* in the Chinese Confucian and Daoist traditions, and to *daya* in Hinduism. This is the closest thing we have to a universal (global) human religious value. It is religion at its best.

The Golden Rule is perhaps the only universal commandment humanity has. It is not a difficult commandment to remember—"Do unto others as you would have others do unto you"; "What is hateful to you, do not do to another"—although it is more difficult to practice than to preach. One scholar has noted that the Golden Rule focuses on oneself and one's own needs first. Instead, he proposes the "Platinum Rule": Do unto others as *they* would have *you* do unto *them*. By following this rule, he suggests, we are required to enter into relationship with the other person and first understand the recipient's needs before acting.[40] His is an important clarification, but however one expresses it, the important thing is to live your version of the Golden Rule because the future of humanity depends on it.[41] Empathize with others. Practice your way of compassion. Help your fellow human beings, whomsoever they are and wherever they may live.

40. Brendan Schulz, TedxYork talk, April 22, 2015.

41. Consider Karen Armstrong's warning delivered at her TED talk in July 2009: "If we don't manage to implement the Golden Rule globally so that we treat all people as though they are as important as ourselves, I doubt we'll have a viable world to hand on to the next generation."

When we follow the way of *hesed*—or *agape, karuna,* and so on—we consciously overcome the separateness and isolation that is bred in each of us. True, we can never surmount life's natural barriers, but by acting in a selfishly selfless way—for that is what the Golden Rule teaches—we are somewhat able to transcend that which separates us one from another. Lovingkindness is the best we are able to offer our fellow creatures, both human and beast, and the rest of Creation. It builds bonds of connection—of unity, love, and trust—and enables us to repair our world.[42]

What I envision as the World to Come is a coming together of people, all committed to creating caring communities. In this World to Come, we each would bring the unique gifts and insights we have acquired during our personal spiritual journeys and the wisdom we have learned from our traditions' teachings, and we would put all this to work in our own distinct ways to build bonds of joy and hope, comfort and consolation and peace, wherever we may live.

Living in this way means to have hope for the future in spite of experience and regardless of one's doubts of either (or both) God and humankind. It means to have faith that by doing acts of lovingkindness, others will be nurtured to do likewise so that, trusting one another, together we may heal our world—ripples of good extending ever outwards, beginning with one simple choice . . .

VI IN CONCLUSION

We need to let go of the past even while we continue to embrace it. We need to let go of tradition even while we cherish it. We need to let go of God while continuing to seek the divine Presence. And we need to see that this Presence inspires the noblest teachings of all faiths and cultures just as surely as it is capable of motivating the best in each of us.

In the end, this is what really matters to me: I *know* that somehow we are all connected and I *know* how I am supposed to conduct myself in this world in order to improve both myself and the world. I continue to have the hope that we can take whatever happens in our lives and transform it into something positive—a blessing—and I have the hope that somehow all we do relates to magnifying our sense of YHVH's presence on this planet.

42. For extended meditations on lovingkindness and its place in our lives, see Fox, *Spirituality Named Compassion* and also Armstrong, *Twelve Steps to a Compassionate Life.*

Mine is a search for people committed to deed, not dogma, although doctrines need not stand in one's way. I personally care less about how God is perceived than that God's presence is felt in a willing and open heart, demonstrated in deeds of caring for one another in the course of daily life, and celebrated in joy and gratefulness. I look for God in how we raise our children and how we treat our fellow human beings and other creatures. Do we treat them with honor and respect or do we shame them, judge them, and punish them? I look for God in whether or not we help others deal with despair and suffering, in whether or not we create hope and spread joy. Ideally what one believes will reinforce one's practice of lovingkindness.

There is only one time to choose to do good and that is now, in the present moment, because the past exists only in memory and the future only in expectations, hopes, and dreams. True, one's choices are influenced by remembrance of things past, and by anxieties for the future, and by self-interest, but the present is all there is, so how one chooses to live on a moment-to-moment basis is really crucial. My rabbinic role model, the sage Hillel, captured some of these competing factors in his famous saying: "If I am not for myself, who is? But if I am only for myself, what am I? And if not now, when?"[43] I ask myself these questions all the time.

What else can I add?

I am now too fast approaching the biblical expiration date of "three-score years and ten," which still defines the human lifespan, and I find myself trying to live a life that continues in this way: by loving my wife and my children, grandchildren, and friends; by looking for the divine in each person and striving to be tolerant and accepting of other people, despite all their *mishugass* (literally "craziness" in Yiddish—but since I'm practicing being tolerant and accepting, let me say "eccentricities"); by acting with compassion and doing deeds of lovingkindness as best I am able; by involving myself in some of the issues facing humanity today; by living a Jewish lifestyle that is personally meaningful to me and my family; by being grateful for life's simple pleasures; and by letting go of God—and letting God grow—in order to remain a Presence in my life.

Writing a book is like having a guest over and spending an evening together. We have spent a number of hours in each other's presence: I through my words and you through your reading and reflection. Hopefully I have not rambled on for too long. But when it's time to close the book and open

43. *Pirkei Avot* 1:14.

the door to see you on your way, I find myself calling out "Wait! I have something more I want to tell you." So here they are, my parting words to you:

Express gratitude.

Practice lovingkindness.

Cultivate your inner bonobo.

Seek YHVH's presence in the world.

Shalom. Salaam. Peace.

Goodbye—and good luck!

Appendix

Laytner's 39 Hypotheses—Or, Where I Am Today

1. YHVH, aka, *Adonai* or "the LORD," also answering to "God," is beyond our comprehension but YHVH's Presence may be perceived by us nonetheless.

2. Because I have experienced it, I know there is a God and, although I don't know what YHVH does, I sense that YHVH is ever changing and somehow good.

3. I choose to endow YHVH with certain qualities, chief among these being some kind of omnipresence. I also most often choose to endow YHVH with a commitment to goodness and justice, a sense of mercy and compassion, some kind of an ability to empathize, and the capacity somehow to engage in some kind of mutual relationship, both individually and collectively.

    a. This may or may not have anything to do with YHVH's reality.

    b. It has a great deal to do with my being a Jew and seeing YHVH through my Jewish lens.

4. My rejection of the traditional conceptions of God in terms of omniscience and omnipotence and traditional male imagery has nothing to do either with YHVH's reality or with my perceived relationship with YHVH.

5. YHVH inspired matter, thereby somehow creating the living, natural world.

6. Like its Source, Creation is dynamic. It is growing, or evolving, and ever changing.

7. I choose to view Creation, like its Source, as tending toward the good in the exercise of its positive potentiality. Toward what end exactly, I cannot know; I may have hopes, but otherwise not a clue.

8. Even though Creation tends toward the good, there are components of it, both great and small, that appear to do harm to other components, simply as a result of their own existence. Disease and death and natural disasters are all part of this process.

9. Nonetheless, although natural "evils" do occur, Creation can still be said to be basically—but not wholly—good.

10. As a Jew, I choose to see life—and human life especially—as growing toward some positive end.

11. As part of Creation, we are basically good.

    a. Nonetheless, we also have the capacity, individually and collectively, to do harm to ourselves, other people, and other parts of Creation.

    b. Part of this capacity is biologically inherited, part imprinted or acquired, and part freely chosen.

    c. Of these determinants, our ability to choose how we act is paramount. We all have free will.

12. We appear to operate (at least some of the time) with a higher level of awareness of our deeds, and with the ability to choose, regardless of the degree of choice involved.

13. The experience of "natural evil" and/or "human evil" is profoundly distressing to most people. Consequently, spirituality—the urge to connect with something greater than ourselves and the need to make sense of the human experience—appears to be a universal aspect of the human condition.

    a. Even so-called secular individuals have these needs, although they may choose to express them without affiliating with a specifically religious group.

14. In response to the spiritual challenges raised by perceived injustice and unwarranted suffering, religions offer to their adherents a variety of explanations, or rationalizations, called theodicies.

15. All theodicies are conjectural, wishful thinking. They are meant more to preserve key aspects of a religion's theology and worldview than to actually comfort the distressed (unless the latter completely believe what they are being told).

16. Theodicies are conjectural because they presume to know more about God and God's *modus operandi* than is humanly possible.

17. YHVH does not intervene directly in history or in human life yet YHVH somehow is a Presence in nature, in human relations, and possibly in the course of history, depending on what paths we individually and collectively choose.

18. YHVH does not respond directly to petitionary prayer. Prayer's value has to do with how it opens us to perceptions of the divine and how it affects our own attitudes and actions.

19. Spirituality is acquired both individually and collectively. It is also expressed both individually and collectively.

20. The collective expressions of spirituality generally are humanity's religions and faith traditions.

    a. Sometimes political movements have substituted for religion.

    b. Sometimes religions have substituted for political movements.

    c. Culture and religion are closely intertwined and often confused with one another.

21. Over time, each religion has developed a distinct perspective on what it believes the divine is or is not. This then becomes its theological reality and institutional foundation.

    a. All religions utilize rituals, beliefs, moral teachings, sacred stories, customs, and art, among other things, with which to express themselves.

    b. Externally, they vary greatly one from another. This is both widely accepted and in many cases actively encouraged so as to promote cohesiveness and identity.

    c. Internally, they vary greatly as well, having changed over time in response to various cultural contexts. Institutional religions, however, tend to minimize this fact and emphasize continuity with the founders instead.

    d. Over time, religions as institutions become focused on ritual and dogma; they ossify. Then renewal movements inject new spirit into the institution and reforms are made—or a split occurs in the institution. Either way, change occurs. This process repeats itself continually.

22. Since each religion operates over many centuries and in diverse geographic locations, its distinct perspective, in fact, is comprised of multiple conceptions of the divine bound together in one mythic whole, regardless of whether or not they contradict one another.

23. Since all religions operate over many centuries and in diverse geographic locations, their distinct perspectives and conceptions either contradict one another *or* they can present a more complete picture of how humanity understands the divine. I choose the latter understanding.

24. One of the goals of institutional religion is to concretize the divine in terms of attributes and activity, so as to make God accessible to clergy and laity through ritual, prayer, study, and deed.

25. Making God accessible unfortunately also means turning YHVH into an idolatrous concept in the sense that YHVH's very indefinability *is* defined and confined by our perceptions, descriptions, expectations, and rituals.

26. It is humanly impossible to avoid the pitfall of wanting to talk about YHVH and making an object of YHVH (unless one chooses not to discuss YHVH at all).

27. Every individual who so chooses may participate in a community of faith, whether through personal search or claimed by inheritance. Regardless, each individual may adapt his/her faith in order to apply it for personal use.

28. Individuals go through stages of spiritual development just as they do physical and emotional development. The former is not necessarily linear, any more than emotional growth is.

29. Religions tend to focus on adherence to belief and practice, and not enough on the process of personal spiritual growth and development. This is because they conflate support of the institution with spirituality.

30. Some religions are based on the concept of revelation. Revelation is a human response to a perception of the divine, although the latter may indeed be a gift.

31. Revelation itself is inspiration but it is content-less. As a human product, it is limited by the abilities, perceptions, expectations, and historical/cultural context(s) of the author(s)/recipient(s).

32. This "original revelation" is built upon by subsequent individuals and generations in a myriad of ways, although the claim of continuity with the original revelation is always maintained. This also conflates the original spiritual experience of the founder(s) with the subsequent religious institution.

33. Some religions are based on one's self-awakening to a "truer reality," a state that also had been disclosed previously to one or more ancient sages.

34. This experience too is conditioned by the abilities, perceptions, expectations, and historical/ cultural contexts both of the "enlightened one" in the past and of later devotees as well.

35. The "enlightening experience" of the founder is also built upon by subsequent individuals and generations in a myriad of ways, although the claim of continuity is likewise maintained. This also conflates the original spiritual experience of the founder(s) with the subsequent religious institution.

36. It appears to be a universal human given to do "good"—and certainly all religions teach the importance of doing "good"—that is, of acting in supportive and helpful ways to one another.

    a. Sometimes this is perceived to be the revealed will of the Creator; sometimes it has been taught by some enlightened sage; or one can say it is just plain common sense for basic survival.

    b. The "Golden Rules" of various religions are the most basic shared expression of this apparent universal human belief and intermittent practice.

37. For most people, the scope of one's "goodness" is limited by self-interest and radiates outward from self to family to kin to clan to community to country.

    a. In some cultures, doing "good" may be limited solely to helping one's own kind, however defined.

    b. In general, however, as long as their personal interests are guaranteed, most people appear willing to do "good" for one another.

38. YHVH is somehow present when people perform acts of lovingkindness and generally follow their version of the Golden Rule. Positive behavior builds the potential for increasing goodness and compassion in human relations and in the course of history, while negative behavior fosters an environment of fear and breeds more negative behavior.

39. The crucial matter is for people of diverse spiritual traditions to recognize that they share more in common than not; and when they are able to put the positive things that they do share into practice, they build up the good and thereby improve the world.

Bibliography

Admirand, Peter. *Amidst Mass Atrocity and the Rubble of Theology: Searching for a Viable Theodicy*. Eugene, OR: Cascade, 2012.

———, editor. *Loss and Hope: Global, Interreligious and Interdisciplinary Perspectives*. London: Bloomsbury, 2014.

Aiken, Lisa. *Why Me, God?: A Jewish Guide for Coping with Suffering*. Northvale, NJ: Aronson, 1996.

Allen, Joel. "Job 3: History of Interpretation." In *Dictionary of the Old Testament: Wisdom, Poetry & Writings*, edited by Tremper Longman and Peter Enns, 361–371. Downers Grove, IL: InterVarsity, 2008.

Allender, Dan B. *The Healing Path: How the Hurts in Your Past Can Lead You to a More Abundant Life*. Colorado Springs, CO: Waterbrook, 1999.

Allender, Dan B., and Tremper Longman. *Cry of the Soul: How Our Emotions Reveal Our Deepest Questions About God*. Colorado Springs, CO: NavPress, 1994.

Armstrong, Karen. *The Great Transformation: The Beginning of Our Religious Traditions*. New York: Anchor, 2007.

———. *Twelve Steps to a Compassionate Life*. New York: Anchor, 2011.

Artson, Bradley Shavit. *God of Becoming and Relationship: The Dynamic Nature of Process Theology*. Woodstock, VT: Jewish Lights, 2013.

Aslan, Resa, and Aaron J. Hahn Tapper, edtiors. *Muslims and Jews in America: Commonalities, Contentions and Complexities*. New York: Palgrave Macmillan, 2011.

Babylonian Talmud (Talmud Bavli). Translated by Maurice Simon et al. New York: Traditional, no date.

Barr, James. "The Question of Religious Influence: The Case of Zoroastrianism, Judaism, and Christianity." *Journal of the American Academy of Religion* 53 (1985) 201–35.

Bartlow, Bruce G. *Medical Care of the Soul: A Practical & Healing Guide to End-of-Life Issues for Families, Patients, & Health Care Providers*. Boulder, CO: Johnson, 2000.

Bass, Diana Butler. *Grounded: Finding God in the World. A Spiritual Revolution*. New York: HarperOne, 2015.

Beverslius, Joel, editor. *Sourcebook of the World's Religions: An Interfaith Guide to Religion and Spirituality*. Novato, CA: New World Library, 2000.

Billman, Kathleen, and Daniel Migliore, *Rachel's Cry: Prayer of Lament and Rebirth of Hope*. Cleveland: United Church, 1999.

Birnbaum, David. *God and Evil: A Unified Theodicy/Theology/Philosophy*. Hoboken: KTAV, 1989.

Blank, Sheldon. "The Prophet as Paradigm." In *Prophetic Thought: Essays and Addresses* 91–101. Cincinnati: Hebrew Union College Press, 1977.

Blumenthal, David R. *Facing the Abusing God: A Theology of Protest.* Louisville: Westminster John Knox, 1993.

Borg, Marcus. *The God We Never Knew: Beyond Dogmatic Religion to a More Authentic Contemporary Faith.* New York: HarperCollins, 1997.

Borowitz, Eugene B. *Renewing the Covenant: A Theology for the Postmodern Jew.* Philadelphia: Jewish Publication Society, 1991.

Boteach, Shmuley. *Wrestling with the Divine: A Jewish Response to Suffering.* Northvale, NJ: Aronson, 1995.

Bowler, Kate. *Everything Happens for a Reason.* New York: Random House, 2018.

Boyce, Mary. *Zoroastrianism: A Shadowy but Powerful Presence in the Judaeo-Christian World.* London: William's Trust, 1987.

Braiterman, Zachary. *(God) After Auschwitz: Tradition and Change in Post-Holocaust Jewish Thought.* Princeton, NJ: Princeton University Press, 1998.

Braude, W. G., translator. *The Midrash on Psalms.* 2 vols. New Haven, CT: Yale University Press, 1959.

———. *Pesikta Rabbati.* 2 vols. New Haven, CT: Yale University Press, 1968.

Brenner, Reeve R. *The Faith and Doubt of Holocaust Survivors.* Northvale, NJ: Aronson, 1997.

Bulka, Reuven P. *Chapters of the Sages: A Psychological Commentary on Pirkey Avoth.* Northvale, NJ: Aronson, 1980.

Burrell, David. *Deconstructing Theodicy: Why Job Has Nothing to Say to the Puzzle of Suffering.* Grand Rapids: Brazos, 2008.

Buxbaum, Yitzhak. *The Life and Teachings of Hillel.* Northvale, NJ: Aronson, 2000.

Callahan, Maggie, and Patricia Kelley. *Final Gifts: Understanding the Special Awareness, Needs, and Communications of the Dying.* New York: Bantam, 1992.

Carroll, James. *Constantine's Sword: The Church and the Jews.* New York: Mariner, 2002.

Clines, David. "The Arguments of Job's Three Friends." In *Art and Meaning: Rhetoric in Biblical Literature,* edited by David Clines et al., 199–214. London and New York: Continuum, 1982.

———. "Why Is There a Book of Job and What Does It Do to You If You Read It?" In *The Book of Job,* edited by Willem A. M. Beuken, 1–20. Bibliotheca Ephemeridum Theologicarum Lovaniensium 114. Leuven: Leuven University Press, 1994.

Cohen, Arthur A., editor. *Arguments and Doctrines: A Reader of Jewish Thinking in the Aftermath of the Holocaust.* New York: Harper and Row, 1970.

Cosgrove, Elliot J., editor. *Jewish Theology in our Time: A New Generation Explores the Foundations and Future of Jewish Belief.* Woodstock, VT: Jewish Lights, 2013.

Crenshaw, James L. *Reading Job: A Literary and Theological Commentary.* Macon, GA: Smyth & Helwys, 2011.

Dawkins, Richard. *The God Delusion.* New York: Houghton Mifflin, 2008.

Dorff, Elliott N., and Louis E. Newman, editors. *Contemporary Jewish Theology: A Reader.* New York: Oxford University Press, 1999.

Eber, Irene. *Chinese and Jews: Encounters Between Cultures.* London: Vallentine Mitchell, 2008.

Ehlich, M.Avrum, editor. *The Jewish-Chinese Nexus: A Meeting of Civilizations.* London: Routledge, 2008.

Ehrman, Bart D. *God's Problem: How the Bible Fails to Answer Our Most Important Question—Why We Suffer*. New York: HarperOne, 2008.

Firestone, Reuven. *Children of Abraham: An Introduction to Islam for Jews*. New York: American Jewish Committee. 2001.

———. *An Introduction to Islam for Jews*. Philadelphia: Jewish Publication Society. 2008.

Fishbane, Michael. *Sacred Attunement: A Jewish Theology*. Chicago: University of Chicago Press, 2008.

———. *Text and Texture: Close Readings of Selected Biblical Texts*. New York: Schocken, 1979.

Fisher, Eugene, editor. *Visions of the Other: Jewish and Christian Theologians Assess the Dialogue*. New York: Paulist, 1994.

Fowler, James W. *Stages of Faith: The Psychology of Human Development and the Quest for Meaning*. Rev. ed. New York: HarperOne, 1995.

Fox, Matthew. *A Spirituality Named Compassion: Uniting Mystical Awareness with Social Justice*. New York: Harper and Row, 1990.

Fretheim, Terence E. *The Suffering of God: An Old Testament Perspective*. Philadelphia: Fortress, 1984.

Friedman, Richard Elliott. *The Disappearance of God: A Divine Mystery*. Boston: Little Brown 1995.

Frymer-Kensky, Tikva, et al. *Christianity in Jewish Terms*. Boulder, CO: Westview, 2000.

Gemser, Berend. "The Rîb—or Controversy—Pattern in Hebrew Mentality." In *Supplement to Vetus Testamentum* 3, 120–37. Leiden: Brill, 1955.

Gibson, John W., and Judy Pigott. *Personal Safety Nets*. Seattle: Classic Day, 2007.

Gilman, Neil. *Sacred Fragments: Recovering Theology for the Modern Jew*. Philadelphia: Jewish Publication Society, 1990.

Glatzer, Nahum N., editor. *Dimensions of Job*. New York: Schocken: 1969.

———. *Hillel the Elder: The Emergence of Classical Judaism*. New York: Schocken, 1966.

———. "Knowest Thou . . . ? Notes on the Book of Job." In *Essays in Jewish Thought*, 82–92. University, AL: University of Alabama Press, 1978.

Goodman, Hananya, editor. *Between Jerusalem and Benares: Comparative Studies in Judaism and Hinduism*. Albany, NY: State University of New York Press, 1994.

Gordis, Robert. *The Book of Job: Commentary, New Translation and Special Studies*. New York: Jewish Theological Seminary, 1978.

Green, Arthur. *Ehyeh: A Kabbalah for Tomorrow*. Woodstock, VT: Jewish Lights, 2003.

———. *Radical Judaism: Rethinking God and Tradition*. New Haven, CT: Yale University Press, 2010.

———. *Seek My Face, Speak My Name*. Northvale, NJ: Aronson, 1992.

Green, James W. *Beyond the Good Death: The Anthropology of Modern Dying*. Philadelphia: University of Pennsylvania Press, 2008.

Greenberg, Irving Yitz. *Cloud of Smoke, Pillar of Fire*. New York: National Jewish Resource Center, 1974.

Griffin, David. *God, Power, and Evil: A Process Theodicy*. Louisville: Westminster John Knox, 2004.

Gruber, Mayer. "Introduction and Annotations to Job." In *The Jewish Study Bible*, edited by Adele Berlin and Marc Zvi Brettler, 1499–1562. New York: Oxford University Press, 2004.

Habel, Norman C. *The Book of Job: A Commentary*. Philadelphia: Westminster, 1985.

————. "The Verdict on/of God at the End of Job." In *Job's God*, edited by Ellen van Wolde, 27–38. London: SCM, 2004.

Harper, Akiba Sullivan, editor. *Langston Hughes Short Stories*. New York: Hill and Wang, 1996.

Harris, Sam. *The End of Faith: Religion, Terror, and the Future of Reason*. New York: Norton, 2004.

Hartley, John. E. "From Lament to Oath: A Study of Progression in the Speeches of Job." In *The Book of Job*, edited by W. A. M. Beuken, 79–100. Bibliotheca Ephemeridum Theologicarum Lovaniensium 114. Leuven: Leuven University Press, 1994.

Hazelton, Lesley. *Agnostic: A Spirited Manifesto*. New York: Riverhead, 2016.

Heifetz, Harold, editor. *Zen and Hasidism*. Wheaton, IL: Quest, 1978.

Heinemann, Joseph. *Prayer in the Talmud: Forms and Patterns*. Berlin and New York: de Gruyter, 1977.

Heller, Joseph. *God Knows*. New York: Dell, 1984.

Herberg, Will. *Judaism and Modern Man: An Interpretation of Jewish Religion*. New York: Meridian, 1959.

Heschel, Susannah, editor. *Abraham Joshua Heschel: Essential Writings*. Maryknoll, NY: Orbis, 2011.

Hitchens, Christopher. *God Is Not Great: How Religion Poisons Everything*. New York: Twelve, 2007.

Humphry, Derek. *Final Exit: The Practicalities of Self-Deliverance and Assisted Suicide for the Dying*. Eugene, OR: Hemlock Society, 1991.

Jacobs, Steven L. *Rethinking Jewish Faith: The Child of a Survivor Responds*. Albany, NY: State University of New York, 1994.

Janzen, J. Gerald. *Job*. Atlanta: John Knox, 1985.

Jaynes, Julian. *The Origins of Consciousness in the Breakdown of the Bi-Cameral Mind*. New York: Houghton Mifflin, 1977.

Jonas, Hans. "The Concept of God After Auschwitz." In *Out of the Whirlwind: A Reader of Holocaust Literature*, edited by Albert Friedlander, 465–76. New York: Schocken, 1976.

Jung, Carl *Answer to Job*. Princeton: Princeton University Press, 1969.

Kamenetz, Roger. *The Jew in the Lotus: A Poet's Rediscovery of Jewish Identity in Buddhism*. San Francisco: HarperSanFrancisco, 1994.

Kasimow, Harold, et al., editors. *Beside Still Waters: Jews, Christians and the Way of the Buddha*. Somerville, MA: Wisdom Publications, 2003.

Katz, Steven, et al., editors. *Wrestling with God: Jewish Theological Responses During and After the Holocaust*. New York: Oxford University Press, 2007.

Kaufmann, Walter. *The Faith of a Heretic*. Garden City, NJ: Anchor, 1963.

Kepnes, Steven. "Job and Post-Holocaust Theodicy." In *Strange Fire: Reading the Bible after the Holocaust*, edited by Tod Linafelt, 252–66. New York: New York University Press, 2000.

Klagsbrun, Francine. *Voices of Wisdom: Jewish Ideals and Ethics for Everyday Living*. New York: Pantheon, 1980.

Kolitz, Zvi, editor. *Yossel Rakover Speaks to God: Holocaust Challenges to Religious Faith*. Hoboken, NJ: KTAV, 1995.

Kraemer, David. *Responses to Suffering in Rabbinic Literature*. New York: Oxford University Press, 1995.

Kugel, James. *The Great Shift: Encountering God in Biblical Times*. Boston: Houghton Mifflin Harcourt, 2017.

Kushner, Harold. *Why Bad Things Happen to Good People*. New York: Avon, 1981.

Lao Tzu. *Tao Te Ching*. Translated by D. C. Lau. Harmondsworth, UK: Penguin, 1963.

Larson, Dale G. *The Helper's Journey: Working with People Facing Grief, Loss, and Life-Threatening Illness*. Champaign, IL: Research Press, 1999.

Laytner, Anson. *Arguing with God: A Jewish Tradition*. Northvale, NJ: Aronson, 1990.

Laytner, Anson, and Jordan Paper, editors. *The Chinese Jews of Kaifeng: A Millennium of Adaptation and Endurance*. Lanham, MD: Lexington, 2017.

Lepore, Jill. "The Commandments: The Constitution and Its worshippers." *The New Yorker*, January 17, 2011, 70–76.

Levine, Amy-Jill, and Marc Zvi Brettler, editors. *The Jewish Annotated New Testament*. New York: Oxford University Press, 2011.

Lobdell, William. *Losing My Religion: How I Lost My Faith Reporting on Religion In America and Found Unexpected Peace*. New York: HarperCollins, 2009.

Lubarsky, Sandra, and David Ray Griffin, editors. *Jewish Theology and Process Thought*. Albany, NY: State University of New York, 1996.

Mackenzie, Don, et al. *Getting to the Heart of Interfaith: The Eye-Opening, Hope-Filled Friendship of a Pastor, a Rabbi and a Sheikh*. Woodstock, VT, Skylight Paths, 2009.

———. *Religion Gone Astray: What We Found at the Heart of Interfaith*. Woodstock, VT: Skylight Paths, 2011.

Mandolfo, Carleen R. *Daughter Zion Talks Back to the Prophets: A Dialogic Theology in the Book of Lamentations*. Atlanta: Society of Biblical Literature, 2007.

———. *God in the Dock: Dialogic Tension in the Psalms of Lament*. Sheffield, UK: Sheffield Academic, 2003.

Michaelson, Jay. *Everything Is God: The Radical Path of Nondual Judaism*. Boston: Trumpeter, 2009.

———. "The Floods in Mississippi: Punishment from an Angry God?" *Forward*, June 3, 2011.

Midrash Rabbah. 11 vols. Edited by Moshe Aryeh Mirkin. Tel Aviv: Yavneh, 1968.

Miles, Jack. *God: A Biography*. New York: Random House, 1995.

Mintz, Alan. *Hurban: Responses to Catastrophe in Hebrew Literature*. New York: Columbia University Press, 1984.

Mitchell, Stephen, translator. *The Book of Job*. New York: Harper Perennial, 1979.

Morinis, Alan. *Climbing Jacob's Ladder: One Man's Journey to Rediscover a Jewish Spiritual Tradition*. New York: Broadway, 2002.

———. *Everyday Holiness: The Jewish Spiritual Path of Mussar*. Boston: Trumpeter, 2007.

Morrow, William S. *Protest against God: The Eclipse of a Biblical Tradition*. Sheffield, UK: Sheffield Phoenix, 2007.

Morse, Melvin L., with Paul Perry. *Closer to the Light: Learning from the Near-Death Experiences of Children*. New York: Random House, 1990.

———. *Parting Visions: Uses and Meanings of Premonitions and After-Death Communications (End of Life Events)*. New York: HarperCollins, 1998.

———. *Transformed by the Light: The Powerful Effects of Near-Death Experiences on Children and Adults*. New York: HarperCollins, 1996.

Neeld, Elizabeth Harper. *Seven Choices: Finding Daylight after Loss Shatters Your World*. New York: Grand Central, 2003.

————. *Tough Transitions: Navigating Your Way Through Difficult Times*. New York: Warner, 2005.

Newman, Louis I. *Hasidic Anthology: Tales and Teachings of the Hasidim*. New York: Schocken, 1963.

Newsom, Carol. *The Book of Job*. New York: Oxford University Press, 2003.

Niebuhr, Gustav. *Beyond Tolerance: How People Across America Are Building Bridges between Faiths*. New York: Penguin, 2008.

Olsvanger, Immanuel. *Contentions with God: A Study in Jewish Folklore*. Capetown: Jewish Historical and Literary Society, 1921.

Ostriker, Alicia Suskin. *For the Love of God: The Bible as an Open Book*. New Brunswick, NJ: Rutgers University Press, 2007.

Paper, Jordan. *The Mystic Experience: A Descriptive and Comparative Analysis*. Albany, NY: State University of New York, 2004.

————. *The Theology of the Chinese Jews, 1000–1850*. Waterloo, ON: Wilfrid Laurier University Press, 2012.

Patt-Shamir, Galia. *To Broaden the Way: A Confucian-Jewish Dialogue*. Lanham, MD: Lexington, 2006.

Perdue, Leo G., and W. Clark Gilpin, editors. *The Voice from the Whirlwind: Interpreting the Book of Job*. Nashville: Abingdon: 1992.

Pesikta Rabbati. Edited by Edward M. Friedmann. Self-published, 1880.

Petuchowski, Jakob J. *Theology and Poetry: Studies in the Medieval Piyyut*. London: Routledge and Kegan Paul, 1978.

Pollak, Michael. *Mandarins, Jews, and Missionaries: The Jewish Experience in the Chinese Empire*. New York: Weatherhill, 1998.

Remen, Rachel Naomi. *Kitchen Table Wisdom: Stories That Heal*. New York: Riverhead, 1996.

Roberts, J. J .M. "Job's Summons to Yahweh: The Exploitation of a Legal Metaphor." *Restoration Quarterly* 16 (1973) 159–65.

Robinson, Anthony B. "Articles of Faith: When Love and Empathy Do Not Right a Wrong." *Seattle Post-Intelligencer*, August 10, 2007.

Romney, Rodney R. "The Changing Faces of God." Sermon, March 13, 2005.

Rosensaft, Menachem Z. "The Days of Awe and the Years of Horror." *Washington Post*, September 11, 2013.

Roskies, David G. *Against the Apocalypse: Responses to Catastrophe in Modern Jewish Culture*. Cambridge, MA: Harvard University Press, 1984.

————, editor. *The Literature of Destruction: Jewish Responses to Catastrophe*. Philadelphia: Jewish Publication Society, 1988.

Rubenstein, Richard L. *After Auschwitz: Radical Theology and Contemporary Judaism*. Indianapolis: Bobbs-Merrill, 1978.

Rudin, A. James. *Ground Rules for Dialogue: A Jewish Guide to Interreligious Relations*. New York: American Jewish Committee, 2006.

Ruether, Rosemary. *Faith and Fratricide: The Theological Roots of Anti-Semitism*. New York: Seabury, 1979.

Rushkoff, Douglas. *Nothing Sacred: The Truth about Judaism*. New York: Three Rivers, 2003.

Sacks, Jonathan. "Bemidbar (5768) – The Wilderness and the Word." *Covenant & Conversation*, May 31, 2008. http://rabbisacks.org/covenant-conversation-5768-bemidbar-the-wilderness-and-the-word-2/.

———. *The Dignity of Difference*. London: Continuum, 2003.

———. *Not in God's Name: Confronting Religious Violence*. New York: Schocken, 2015.

Schiff, Daniel. "Reimagining Torah." *CCAR Journal* 41:3 (Summer 1994) 49–64.

Scholnick, Sylvia Huberman. "Lawsuit Drama in the Book of Job." PhD diss., Brandeis University, 1975.

Schraub, J. Jonathan. "For the Sin We Have Committed by Theological Rationalizations: Rescuing Job from Normative Religion." *Soundings* 86:3–4 (Fall/Winter 2003) 439–42.

Schulweis, Harold M. *For Those Who Can't Believe: Overcoming Obstacles to Faith*. New York: Harper Collins, 1994.

Schwartz, Howard, and Anthony Rudolf, editors. *Voices within the Ark: The Modern Jewish Poets*. New York: Avon, 1980.

Silverman, Jason M. *Persepolis and Jerusalem: Iranian Influence on the Apocalyptic Hermeneutic*. Library of Hebrew Bible/Old Testament Studies 558. London: T. & T. Clark, 2012.

Singer, Ellen, editor. *Paradigm Shift: From the Jewish Renewal Teachings of Reb Zalman Schachter-Shalomi*. Northvale, NJ: Aronson, 1993.

Sinn, Simone, and Michael Reid Trice, editors. *Religious Identity and Renewal: Jewish, Christian and Muslim Explorations*. Leipzig: Evangelishce Verlagsanstalt, 2015.

Soloff, Rav "My God." *CCAR Journal* 46:1 (Winter 1999) 56–66.

Soloveitchik, Joseph. "Confrontation." *Tradition: A Journal of Orthodox Thought* 6:2 (1964) 5–29.

Sommer, Benjamin D. *Revelation and Authority: Sinai in Jewish Scripture and Tradition*. New Haven, CT: Yale University Press, 2016.

Spong, John Shelby. *Liberating the Gospels: Reading the Bible with Jewish Eyes*. San Francisco: HarperSanFrancisco, 1996.

———. *Why Christianity Must Change or Die: A Bishop Speaks to Believers in Exile*. San Francisco: HarperSanFrancisco, 1998.

Steindl-Rast, David. *Common Sense Spirituality: The Essential Wisdom of David Steindl-Rast*. New York: Crossroad, 2008.

———. *Gratefulness, the Heart of Prayer: An Approach to Life in Fullness*. New York: Paulist, 1984.

Stern, Sholom. *When Words Fail: A Religious Response to Undeserved Hurt*. Northvale, NJ: Aronson, 1999.

Stone, Ira F. *A Responsible Life: The Spiritual Path of Mussar*. New York: Aviv, 2006.

Sutherland, Robert. *Putting God on Trial: The Biblical Book of Job*. Victoria, BC: Trafford, 2004.

Swidler, Leonard. "The Dialogue Decalogue." *Journal of Ecumenical Studies* 20:1 (1983) 1–4.

———, et al. *Trialogue: Jews, Christians, and Muslims in Dialogue*. New London, CT: Twenty Third Publications, 2007.

Swinton, John. *Raging with Compassion: Pastoral Responses to the Problem of Evil*. Grand Rapids: Eerdmans, 2007.

Talmage, Frank E., editor. *Disputation and Dialogue: Readings in the Jewish Christian Encounter*. New York: KTAV, 1975.

Talmud Bavli (Babylonian Talmud). 12 vols. Vilna: Rom, 1912.

Tanakh: The Holy Scriptures: The New JPS Translation According to the Traditional Hebrew Text. Philadelphia: Jewish Publication Society, 1988.

Teasdale, Wayne. *The Mystic Heart: Discovering a Universal Spirituality in the World's Religions*. Novato, CA: New World, 2001.

Tsevat, Matitiahu. "The Meaning of the Book of Job." *Hebrew Union College Annual* 37 (1966) 73–106.

Twain, Mark. *Letters from the Earth*. Edited by Bernard DeVoto. New York: Crest, 1963.

Ullendorf, Edward. "Thought Categories in the Hebrew Bible." In *Studies in Rationalism, Judaism and Universalism*, edited by Raphael Loewe, 273–88. London: Routledge and Kegan Paul, 1966.

Vandeman, Helen. *We Are One: Using Intuition to Awaken to Truth*. New York: iUniverse, 2002.

Viorst, Judith. *Necessary Losses: The Loves, Illusions, Dependencies and Impossible Expectations That All of Us Have to Give Up in Order to Grow*. New York: Fawcett Gold Medal, 1986.

Wade, Nicholas. *The Faith Instinct: How Religion Evolved and Why It Endures*. New York: Penguin, 2009.

Walton, John H. "Book of Job I." In *Dictionary of the Old Testament: Wisdom, Poetry & Writings*, edited by Tremper Longman and Peter Enns, 333–46. Downers Grove, IL: InterVarsity, 2008.

Weiss, Dov. *Pious Irreverence: Confronting God in Rabbinic Judaism*. Philadelphia: University of Pennsylvania Press, 2017.

Weisz, Tiberiu. *The Covenant and the Mandate of Heaven: An In-Depth Comparative Cultural Study of Judaism and China*. New York: iUniverse, 2008.

Wels-Schon, Greta. *Portrait of Yahweh as a Young God, or How to Get Along with a God You Don't Necessarily Like but Can't Help Loving*. New York: Holt Rinehard and Winston, 1968.

Westermann, Claus. *The Structure of the Book of Job: A Form-Critical Analysis*. Philadelphia: Fortress, 1981.

White, William Charles. *Chinese Jews*. 2nd ed. Toronto: University of Toronto Press, 1966.

Whitney, Barry. *What Are They Saying about God and Evil?* New York: Paulist, 1989.

Williamson, Marianne. *A Return to Love: Reflections on the Principles of* A Course In Miracles. New York: HarperCollins, 1992.

Winkler, Gershon, and Lakme Batya Elior. *The Place Where You Are Standing Is Holy: A Jewish Theology on Human Relationships*. Northvale, NJ: Aronson, 1994.

Wolde, Ellen J. van. "Job 42, 1–6: The Reversal of Job." In *The Book of Job*, edited by Willem A. M. Beuken, 223–50. Bibliotheca Ephemeridum Theologicarum Lovaniensium 114. Leuven: Leuven University Press, 1994.

Wood, James. "Holiday in Hellmouth: God May Be Dead, but the Question of Why He Permits Suffering Lives On." *New Yorker*, June 9 and 16, 2008.

Wright, Robert. *The Evolution of God*. New York: Little, Brown, 2009.

Zaehner, Richard C. *The Comparison of Religions*. Boston: Beacon, 1959.

Zuckerman, Bruce. *Job the Silent: A Study in Historical Counterpoint*. New York: Oxford University Press, 1991.

Index